Afternoon
Tea with
Sensei

Afternoon Tea with Sensei

KATHY HALER

To order additional copies of this book, contact:
Xlibris Corporation
0-800-644-6988
www.xlibrispublishing.co.uk
Orders@xlibrispublishing.co.uk
302204

Contents

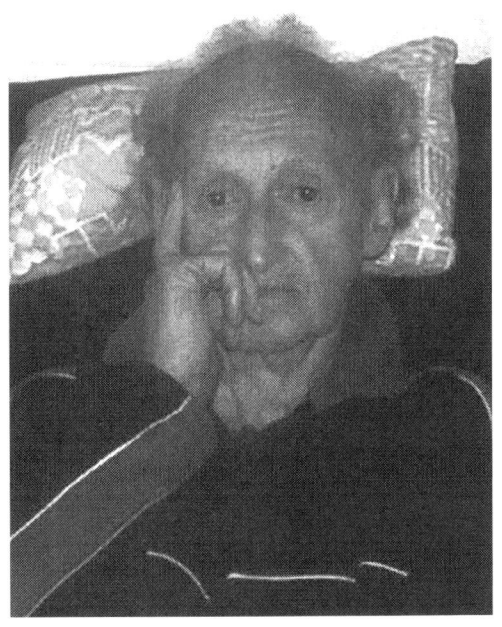

We lay this little book at the Feet of Sensei, a Yogi in a
track-suit. Who has sat with great patience on many boulders
with us and even lifting the boulders that have sat on us. A
man of pure integrity, whose selfless service to humanity has
guided many a person back to their path.

To the compassionate destroyer
Thank you.

Steadman Davies, MBE

Preface

Introduction to Sensei.

The first part of this little book is a question. Who is this Sensei?

Afternoon tea with Sensei.

The second part of this little book is full of questions and answers. Questions that anyone could have asked, but only a few could answer with such clarity, such simplicity, and with the understanding of the authentic Truth.

(The captions in bold at the end of each sections are sayings. Sensei's sayings, which Sensei frequently says during the class. These sayings have travelled down with him through the years and are his teachings.)

Yoga starts in the belly.

In the third part of this little book, are some of his teachings on different subjects that we have asked him to explain, in words that we could understand and therefore grasp the deeper meaning, or at least feel it. We hope you find in this little book, what we found, as we listened to him.

Softening,

The fourth part of this little book, takes us through the three practises
that Sensei teaches.
The practise of softening.
The practise with the inner-breath.
The practise of keeping the centre line clear.
And the seed-mantras for the six centres in the centre-line.

Jesus.

The fifth part of this little book holds
a small gathering of Sensei's teachings about Jesus.

(Note. If you were to read about Jesus, read from the oldest version of the
New Testament you can find.)

A Short introduction to Sensei

Question: Who is this Sensei? That is the question!

And this little book does not answer it, but here are some facts.

Facts: Sensei was born in Wales in the year 1925 in a village called Bwlch-Y-Gwynt that is now part of Llanelli. The main work in the area at that time was in the TinPlate Factory and religion was deeply woven into the very fabric of life. People seemed closer and there was a deep sense of community. Sensei was an only child and his mother died when he was about two. His father also left due to a family matter so he was brought up by his Gran and an Auntie. He grew up in a working, loving and large family. His birth name is David Steadman Davies, but to many he is known as just Steadman, to others as Di Yogi and to some as Sensei. There are not many people in Llanelli who have not heard of, or come to that, who have not had some contact with Sensei. Either through the martial arts, yoga and meditation. Let alone through his silent caring for humanity. Sensei left school at the age of fourteen, and worked as a framer of boxes. When asked how old he was when he understood who he was, Sensei said he had always known something, but was not aware of what he knew. It was when he was a young man that the inner-knowledge started to flow. He said there had to be time for preparing. But he did say that he had found it frustrating as a young man, for there was no literature or people he could talk to about Sai Baba. Both Sensei and Sai Baba were young men back then.

Sensei joined the army at the age of eighteen and was based in India. Sensei said "My job was not to get into a war." He had never been in a battle, and just for the record, he is very silent about that phase of his life, it's like getting blood out of a stone, hard work. Although there is a story about how he was shot in the back and the bullet past right through him. He should have died but it is said that he felt the Ki in his belly and knew he would be ok. When asked about this story, he just said "something like that". He is known as a man of few words!

Sensei has spoken of the time when he and a friend were sitting in line in a Dojo in Korea. It was in this Dojo he was taught the martial arts. There where many sitting in line, and the Japanese Master of the Dojo in Korea stopped in front of them and said "Christians!" They answer with a yes, knowing that they were probably the only ones. The Japanese Master said "Good! read John chapter 7 verse 38, As the scripture says, Whoever believes in me, streams of life-giving water will pour out from his belly,: This is what you are practicing to do." He also speaks of a time when he was in India and staying in an army camp near a village called Ranchi, his tent was situated right at the far end of this massive camp, in a corner. Just over the wall was an ashram and he used to sit on this wall watching the ashram's people practicing their yoga. It was in this ashram that Sensei first started to practice yoga. Another ashram he was posted near to was Sai Baba's ashram. When he heard that Sai Baba was an Avatar, God in human form, he knew that this was the Truth, there was no doubt within him. God is on earth.

Sensei said that he learnt more about Jesus while he was in Korea and India than he did from all his church activates at home. He has said that the Christians have painted a lovely picture of the Christian religion, but they have not shown how to get into the picture! Sensei too many, is Llanelli's Yogi Saint and these are some of his teachings we have had the privilege to hear.

Afternoon Tea with Sensei.

Afternoon Tea with Sensei.

Afternoon tea with Sensei, 22-11-07.

Question: How did it all start, where did God come from?. *Answer.* First there was Knowledge, Knowledge holds everything there is to become or not to become, everything that has become or not become, and everything that will become or not become. There is nothing that is not held within Knowledge, but Knowledge was not doing anything. Knowledge just was. Imagine a very big shoal of thousands of tiny fish, all moving one way in a great swarm then shooting of in another and then another. This image can help you visualize Knowledge if an image helps, but Knowledge has no form, but holds with in it the seed of all forms and none-forms. Knowledge felt the urge to Become, to experience Its Self. Within Knowledge was the seed principle of Love. God came into Being when the seed of Love spouted out of the urge to Become which was held within Knowledge. God is Love and Love is God. Love is the creating principle behind all of creation. God created the Universe and beyond out of Love, for that is the nature of God. It was only the Love Principle within Knowledge that could make use of Knowledge. God is Love, God planted His Own Self into creation and it grew. All knowledge is outside, but to know, you have to move inwards. God and Knowledge are One not two. God is the manifestation of Knowledge. In deep contemplation, knowledge comes in. Great Scientists have been known to say that the answer/ knowledge they were seeking just came by itself while they were deep in thought. The heart centre (anahata chakra, unstruck sound) is the receiver. Knowledge received in heart centre moves to the solar-plexus, before entering the brain. The brain cannot think, feel, or love, (creating principle). The brain is a library, a memory bank. The hara, (sea of consciousness) is held within the belly, develop it and all fear will go. When the belly is full, there is no room for anger. (Sensei had no word to describe what happens when all fears leave the sea of consciousness.) We control ourselves not in the head, but in the belly.

Sensei often states that nothing can be brought into being without Love being at the root of its cause.

Soften, soften, soften.
Afternoon tea with Sensei on 29-11-07.

Sensei: You have to go in! to come out. Within us is the machinery that enables us to accept and experience what is on the outside. Cars can not be driven on the outside; you have to go inside the car to drive it. The heart centre, (anahata chakra, unstuck sound) is the receiver. The other centre/chakras are power houses. (There are six chakras rooted in the sushumna, which is a column of energy within the spine) We have enough fuel (energy) inside of us for living, but we need to fill up the tank, to enable us to move inwards, to extend outwards.

Question: When you have a vision of Baba, does Baba send the vision from India or heaven or Knowledge. Where does that vision come from?

Answer: Baba (God) comes out of the heart centre (anahata). If you have a vision of Baba, or any form of God. God has come out of your heart centre. He gives a nudge from inside and comes outside. You need a key to turn the power on; softening is the keys. The power inside creates the illusion outside. If inside is disorientated, the outside will be a disorientated illusion. Mind comes in! There are only seven notes and nine numbers.

All music, all sound come from these seven notes. Why only seven? From a child's nursery rhymes to a full blown symphony there is only seven notes within it. All mathematics arises from the same nine numbers. God did not create an eighth note or a tenth number. Why? Ask Baba. There is a story of how the people from a fishing village went to Baba and asked "Why have all the fish gone?" Baba told them that their ancestors use to pray to the sea god. Find out how your ancestors use to pray. Prayer is concentrated power that comes from inside. Man has forgotten how to pray. Meditation is a key. Thomas Edison (a famous scientist of the ninetieth century) said he actual felt the knowledge coming into him when he was in deep contemplation. Yoga helps to open up, to receive. Softening and feeling create more space for the energy/ prana to enter in and strike the switches of the power houses, (chakras). OM is the underlying sound that is within all of creation. It is the sound of creation. The inner journey takes you to OM. OM is deep within the heart centre, (anahata, unstruck sound). When struck, Sensei then just shrugged his shoulders and looks as if to say, "It can only be experienced". Mike, who had joined us, spoke of the time a member of the Dojo heard the sound of OM for the first time. Mike explained that Sensei and Dorothy were coming off the mat and as they walked through the door, the sound of OM came with them. Sensei parting words that day were. "Nothing outside of you can die!"

Yoga starts in the belly.
Evening class with Sensei on Tuesday, 4-12-07.

Sensei: Knowledge always has been and always will be. Until experienced, no explanation will satisfy Nothing outside of you can die, all is Spirit. All is Knowledge, but where is it? It is all around, but you can't see it, it is everywhere. It is where God gets His information from. God planted His Own Self in creation. Brahman (Primal source, God) unmanifested, is you! We are all unmanifested parts of Brahman. When you know that, you are manifested Brahman, God. Sathya Sai Baba knows He is God. In His previous life as Shirdi Baba, His

Knowledge was not complete. He had held some things back. In this life as Sri Sathya Sai Baba, He has come as a Full-blown Avatar with all Knowledge of past, present and future at His finger-tips. Shakti, (Divine Energy) is at His Will, and all of creation within His Being. Within Knowledge all exists in seed form. Good is innate, bad is scattered around. The feeling of sacredness needs to flow again. Love is the source of all creation, nothing can come into creation with out Love as it's source. Scientists can only create things out of the elements or things that are already created. They can take a bit of this and a bit that, mix them together and bring something out of Gods creation. Knowledge and Love are the basis of Creation, what we do, or have done with creation is, or has been our choice. Love is the Primal Cause of Creation.

Teach the mind to feel
Evening class with Sensei, 11.12.07.

Sensei: Everything comes through process. Spirit is One, soul individual. People have more experiences than they remember! Through the power of reason, slowly we become more human. Animals have souls and different animals have certain inborn characteristics, such as the characteristics of a herd animal or a carnivore. A soul embodied within the animal earns the right, through the continuous evolution of that soul to take on the highest form of animal, a man or woman. The characteristic of the animal that soul last embodied will come with the soul when it reincarnates. These characteristic can help aid a soul, as it evolves from being a soul within an animal/human, to a soul within a human being, an embodied soul that remembers its innate divinity? God planted His Knowledge in man.

            Howard told us of a dream his son had. At the end of this dream vision, a Native American Indian appeared, and when the Indian had finished his teachings to the young man, the Indian said "Give my regards to Sensei". Sensei was chuckling.

Feel, don't think so much.
Afternoon tea with Sensei. Thursday 13.12.07.

Of course, the *question* arose: "Who was that Indian in the dream?"

Answer: After a wait, the answer came. He is a Hopi Indian called Running Water. Hopi Indian's are very spiritual.

Question: Is he still in the world or is he in spirit?

Answer: He is in the world.

Question: Are there many people in the world like you and this Indian?

Answer: More than you think. (pause) After Sathya Sai Baba, Prema Sai will come. Prema Sai (the last in the Trinity, Shirdi Sai, Sathya Sai and Prema Sai) will not come as a Full Blown Avatar for He will not need all that He needs now in this Incarnation. He would have already taken on the heaviest load of karma and the human race would be back on the path, the path of right-living, compassion, truth, and no-violence. The last Full-blown Avatar was Krishna. (5,000 years ago) Avatars bring only what is needed. Shirdi Sai did not need all that Sathya Sai brought with Him this time round. Sathya Sai Baba is the sum total of everything!

Question: What is the difference between a realized soul and an Avatar?

Answer: A realized soul is moving inwards but not all in. Avatar is all in! Realization starts when you first look inwards. Some sort of experience is needed to turn the soul inwards. Before the experience, the soul was outward looking.

Question: Sometimes we can feel very close to true understanding, to self-realization and then the next moment it can feel it will take eternity and a day, why?

Answer: A sigh! You are moving forward, then for some reason or another you let out a long deep audible breath of weariness, a sigh of dispiritedness. You slide back with that sigh and when the sighing stops and you are ready again, you have to first recover the ground you have already walked. You could have just been about to knock on the door, or may be you had knocked on the door and nobody came, so you knocked again and may be again and may be you let out a sigh of impatientness. That sigh drains your power to stay at the door or even on the path! How much it drains you depends on how big the sigh. Many people don't know how close they are or have been to knocking at the door.

Here is a little illustration. You see a marvelous program on the television, it inspires you while you are watching it, when the program is finished, you turn the television off, but you do not do anything about what you saw in that program that touched you, that made an impression on you. The program slips into the back of your mind and is forgotten. Then some months later, that television program comes to the forefront of your mind and again you are inspired, so you go to the library or a book shop to look for a book on the subject. The book tells you to go to certain places. "Ok," you thought. You even found out where the Yoga school was, but you did not go for some reason. Maybe Mary was going with you but she decides not to go, so you don't go. Later on in the year or may be even the year after, the old book popped up again, "dam it!" you say to yourselves "I am going to Yoga". You went to the yoga class and knocked on the door of the Dojo, but turned back before anyone inside could open the door, with a sigh of "may be I am not quite ready for this." Time moves on and the old book starts making more sense to you. You become more interested so you go back to the Yoga school, and this time you wait till someone opens the door. You asked one of the members what nights they practice on. But on the nights they practice, you were always busy. A few more months came and went before you were once again at the Yoga school. You were in the foyer talking to one of the members and you saw a class on the mat practicing their positions. With a sigh thought of "I could never do that!" You asked the member who was explaining things to you "if there was any other way?" You went back home with a heavy feeling, but all the while you were improving, even though you did not know it. Time goes on and the book was left alone, until one day you came across the book again and it up-lifted you. So off you went to the Yoga school with the determination that you would go on the mat! On the mat you get on well with the other members, and at last you feel like you are on the path. It is fear of changes and self-doubt that creates and gives power to a sigh. Self-confidence, fortitude, and determination give no room for the sighs of weariness and dispiritedness. Sighs make you weak, softening makes you strong. Jesus said "The road is long and narrow," but we have to find the road. He did not tell us where it is. Patience is a must if you want to stop sighing.

Question: I don't know what self-realization is, what happens when you become self-realized?

Answer: Slightly different for all of us. Why did I find it through martial arts? Christian monks were also once taught the Martail arts, using the staff or the sword.

Question: Does healing come from inside or outside?

Answer: Healing comes from outside. Healing enters through the medullar into the heart centre (*Anahata*) then out. You draw in energy through the medullar. The heart centre is the receiver. Everything from outside, goes first to the heart centre. All knowledge is outside. God (Love principle) took from Knowledge what was needed and placed it in mankind and still is! You can feel knowledge enter; it is not through thinking. It is feeling. We learn to feel our way. All knowledge first enters the heart centre, then moves to the solar-plexus before in moves into the brain, that is when the arguments starts. Knowledge always was. God (Love principle) was always within Knowledge (as seed form) and always will be. God grew with the Knowledge It drew into Itself.

Question: We talk of lower-self and higher-self. Are there two selves within us?

Answer: No two selves, no higher or lower, only oneself. The inner play of what we call the higher-self and lower-self, is just the Self finding out about Itself and deciding what it would like to be and finding out what it is not. It is the play of duality within. Self-realization is no duality, just Self. We practice to rise above, to move beyond duality to Oneness. See beyond duality. Duality is the Law of attraction and repulsion. We rise above the Law of attraction and repulsion. Pain and pleasure are creations of the mind. Pain is bad and pleasure is good or so it seems. The pleasure of eating too much causes pain and pain can be a warning of something is wrong. All comes from the One seed of God in Knowledge.

Question: About the Hopi Indian, have you met?

Answer: Yes and No. How can we comprehend the evolution of the soul? From before time, we were. Our first form was millions of years ago, at the beginning of time.

Afternoon tea with Sensei many moons ago.

Question: Is the atma what we call the soul?

Answer: Yes and no. (A typical reply)

Question: Is Atma the Soul of the soul?

Answer: Yes, you could put it like that.

Afternoon tea with Sensei. 10.1.08.

Question: Is the soul/atma in animals the same as in people?

Answer: Yes, no difference.

Question: Does a soul, that has left an animal body, say due to a car crash get confused, like a soul that leaves a human body in a similar situation can.

Answer: Yes, animals feel the same as humans. Animal, all animals can love. Look at animals! Animals are amazing.

Feel, you will never get yoga by thinking.
Afternoon tea with Sensei, 17.1.08.

Question: I read that Baba said that when the mind is transparent and pure, your true self will know itself. Does that mean that the mind becomes a mirror for the true self to know itself?

Answer: Do you know how much is in our minds. The thoughts we have put into the mind! It's not so much know itself, but as our minds become clearer, the yearning of the self to be known, is felt.

Question: How can we clear our minds? Is it by turning the direction of our focus inwards, towards the self therefore ignoring the mind and its games?

Answer: That is what the practice is about, doing a complete turn around. We may hear a word or two that pulls us back on to the inner path, although we might not have realized that we were or had slipped off it. Our thoughts were pulling us off the path. Our own thoughts could become our worse enemies, specially the ones we put in a long time ago. Sometimes, you can feel your own thoughts pulling you off the path. Doubting thoughts are the worse enemies. It is much harder now days, much harder. Things pull from all directions.

Question: Last week while I was on the mat, I was contemplating on Oneness and although I have contemplated this many times, thinking that we are all one. That time, I felt it completely.

Answer: Yes, and as you carry on with the practice of softening you will start to feel infinity not only with people, but with animals.

Question: If in essence we are the same, and The Divine loves us all the same. Has always and will always. Why practice?

Answer: To give you strength to carry on, to move forward, to reach the goal. Afternoon tea was coming to a close when Sensei said "You are still pondering over what I said before. 'Nothing outside of you can die'. He then added, with that smile playing on his face, "You have to go in to die".

Feel your way in.
Afternoon tea with Sensei, 24.1.08.

On the way to the cafe Sensei was looking up and said, half to himself "The clouds have gone, were have they gone too?"

Question: I was talking to Sensei about a nature program I had seen on the television. It was a beautiful program and the narrator was a man called Satish Kumar. I said, "There is so much beauty in nature, you could get lost in it.

Answer: Of course.

Question: I read an article that said the mind and the brain are not separate but the same. To think that they are separate is Gnostic that went out with the Dark Age.

Answer: Babies are not born with their brains full. Their brains are empty. Things are put into their brains. The brain is a memory bank. Mind is outside. Mind comes in.

Question: Does not the mind come with the baby?

Answer: No. The mind is outside, mind comes in.

Question: Then what is it that is brought forward from one life cycle to the next?

Answer: That which is to do with the soul.

Question: The mind, the everyday part of the mind is cluttered and over flowing with all sorts of things. I have started the practice of focusing my mind on my forehead centre (*Ajna chakra seat of the buddhi/ Intellect, seat of discrimination and reasoning*) with the hope that I can move away from the clutter of rubbish that seems to fill it at times, (too many times) Is this right?

Answer: Yes. The mind is everywhere and we have to learn how to sort out what is needed and what is not. What we refer to as our mind is just a tiny speck of the Universal mind

Question: Has Baba taken on individual karma or collective /world karma?

Answer: All karma.

Question: I was thinking about this the other day, and it felt to me that Baba takes the karma into Himself, purifies it, then release it back as pure energy. Is this what happens?

Answer: Yes, Baba takes on all karma that is why His body suffers.

Slow deep breathing in the belly.
Afternoon tea with Sensei. 31-1-08.

I was talking to Sensei about a program on the television the other night that spoke about Cuba and how the Cuban people had pulled together as a society. The people of Cuba now grow their own food and medicine, and speak of the years after Russia left, as the twelve special years. They are creating a stable friendly environmental system based on people power that cares. Mike, who was with us said, "Yes, and the same is happening in Russia. Baba removed the dark heavy cloud of negative thoughts that was hanging over Russia". Mike's exact words were "Baba blew it to smithereens: I was over Norway at the time". Much was said by Mike, many things were explained, but I can't find the words, they'll come, but until then, I will sum it up as best I can. Mike explained that Sai Baba is here for The Creation, the whole of Creation. That is His job. He will not leave The Creation, which is His manifested. Sensei and Mike work in the unmanifested. What ever happens in the unmanifested, will have its affects on the manifested. Mike also said that you can hear a soul descending into creation. There is a sizzling noise, but when it leaves, the soul leaves in stillness.

Question: Is Earth the lowest place to go?
Answer: Yes.

[Sensei's confirmed what Mike was saying, not with words but with the look within his eyes, and subtle nods of his head, until he said "It's time to go". Mike replied, "That's telling me to shut-up".

Sensei said "No it's not", but it was time to go.

Belly falls in as you breathe out.
Afternoon tea with Sensei. 7-2-08.

I asked Sensei to read an article in the Metro paper. It was about some scientists who claimed to be very close to time traveling. They said that soon they would be able to blast a hole to create a worm tunnel in space, so that people from the future will be able to travel back in time, but only to the time the worm hole was created. Sensei after reading it said "I don't think they will be able to do that". A few moments past then Sensei said, "Where are they thinking of putting the hole?" (This was soon followed by). "They have no understanding of the forces that are out there. The power is beyond them".

Sensei then spoke about the soul having to pass through many, (beyond count) life forms. How a soul has taken on life forms that only live for a few seconds, why? And what linage do we come from? He finished of by putting a question to me. "Why did God feel that it was necessary for the soul to pass through thousands of different life form, such as insects, plants, fish, birds, and animals? Could there have been another way? Ask Baba next time you see Him".

I mentioned Genesis, and how it states that Adam and Eve were thrown out of the Garden of Eden because they ate the forbidden fruit from the Tree of Knowledge. Sensei said "The Tree of Knowledge is where God takes what He needs".

Question: It is said that God planted His knowledge in man. Why does it then say that man was turned out of the Garden because he ate the fruit from the Tree of Knowledge?
Answer: Sensei just shrugs his shoulders.
Question: Why does a soul make a sizzling sound when it is entering the material plane, but leaves in stillness?

Answer: (after some thoughtful silence). That is a hard question.
Question: Could it be likened to a meteorite entering the Earth atmosphere and burning up?
Answer: Yes, you could put it like that.
Question: Meteorites are usually very big in space but by he time they enter the Earth's atmosphere they are tiny.
Question: Say it is a soul of a saint that is entering the material plane, would the sizzling sound be of a higher vibration?
Answer: No, it would be quieter.

Belly expands as you breathe in.
Afternoon tea with Sensei, 14-2-08.

After last week's, afternoon tea with Sensei, I picked up a Sai book and read these lines.

> *Man consumes as food many living beings, plants, eggs, fish, cattle, sheep etc. They are born as human beings, on account of this consumption. But, since they have not had the education which can reveal the God within they vegetate or stay brutish, without appropriate ticket or passport for rising higher than the human status in which they have been hurriedly placed.* So I went to tea this afternoon with these words from Baba.

Question: Is it because the soul needs to pass though the countless forms of different beings, living forms, so that it can accumulate experiences beyond our comprehension, and therefore grow in knowledge. Does the evolution of the soul grow with these experiences of life in form?
Answer: Definitely.

Keep the inner-breath in the belly.
Afternoon tea with Sensei, 21-2-08.

Question: I have only heard you say "Nothing outside of you can die", until I read in the Sai book last night these words. *The Universal of which you are a unit is pure, true, egoless, unlimited and everlasting. Contemplate on It and your innate egolessness, truth, purity, and eternality will manifest itself, more and more everyday.*

Does that mean everything that my physical eyes see, every single particle of the physical world, the Universe, is a part of God, the manifestation of God? Therefore It is God and as God is eternal, nothing can die.

Answer: God can die. (I was not expecting that answer; I was expecting a 'yes, of course').

Question: (after a stun silence) do you mean by 'God dies', that God will merge back into Himself, His Unmanifested Self?

Answer: No, as far as we are concerned, God dies, Krishna died. Find yourself first, and then you will find God. (Using his hand to add vision to his words,) Sensei then said "soften, soften, soften", while bringing his finger tips slowly together until they touched with one last gentle "soften", taking me inwards.

Question: It seems as if our world is on the lowest level of manifestation, there is nothing, so to speak, beneath it. Is there a hell?

Answer: Yes, hell is inside of you. You, torment yourself. Both heaven and hell are with in you.

Question: Some people live through the horrors of war or terrorism. Terrorism even within their so called families they live with. It must feel like hell. It is said that it is due to karma, but how can you say, lets say to a mother, "Your baby has died due to karma", whether the cause was a disorder within the baby or a bomb.

Answer: Sensei placed three objects in a line on the table. The first represented a stillborn baby, the second represented a baby who lived only for a day, and the third represented a baby that lived for a week. Sensei explained that the souls of those babies knew that they were only coming for such a short time. That was all they needed, but of course you can not tell a mother that, for she is in to much pain and confusion.

Question: I am not worried about myself. I know I am facing the right way and on the homeward path. I need only to sit and do the practice, there is no more search, just waiting. But what about the rest of us? We have got so caught up, so wrapped up that when you look into it, it seems impossible to untangle the knots.

Answer: I feel that in the year 2012 or there about, Baba will do
              something so magnificence in its grandeur and beneficence
              that people will stop and turn around.

Learn to feel.
Afternoon tea with Sensei, 6-3-08.

Question: With the aid of a scan they can pick up an image of a baby
              of five weeks. It is like, (I've been told) a tiny bubble with a
              minute black speck within it. This black speck is the heart of
              the newly being formed baby. At about six weeks the black
              speck seems to move, this movement is the tiny vibration of a
              minute heart beat. Does the soul enter the newly forming baby
              when the heart gives its first beat?

Answer: No. The baby is three to four weeks old before the soul has
              fully entered, but Spirit is there.

Question: What is the difference between consciousness and mind?

Answer: Consciousness feels, mind does not. Consciousness is life, mind
              is not. Mind is everywhere; you can pick up bits of mind from
              all over the place. Consciousness is inside, mind is outside,
              mind comes in.

Question: Is what we refer to as life force consciousness?

Answer: No, life force is pure energy. Consciousness, life force and mind
              are different, but they are one.

There is no limit to the softening, don't make one.
Evening class with Sensei, 11-3-08.

Question: When a Great Soul takes on a human form, does it take longer
              for the Soul of that Great Being to become fully manifested
              with in the human form? Is it the Greater the Soul, the longer
              it takes?

Answer: No, it takes three to four weeks for any soul to fully enter a
              human form.

Question: Why is it that the Great Beings seem to manifest their Truth
              around the age of fourteen?

Answer: They throw off their childhood around that time, (then with a chuckle) although I was already working at the age of twelve.

Question: Can we have control of our dreams and if so, how?

Answer: No, you just sit and watch them, a bit like a movie. You are just watching all the tricks, the pranks and the games that the little part of you that is looking outwards gets up to. Why?

Question: I have had some strange dreams of late. Do our dreams reflect our state of mind?

Answer: No, although our waking life does come in to our dreams. I remember a dream I had when I was a boy of nine. I was running with a group of boys from the village and a farmer was chasing us. I just escaped through the hedge. I could feel his hand, his fingers were clawing at my shoulder trying to get a hold on me but I managed to slip through the hedge. During that day I had been on the other side (across the railway,) with my Auntie and when we arrived back home I saw the group of boys running. I joined in because I thought it was a game of chase and I did not want to be the chaser. I did not know they had been up to some mischief and a farmer was after them and he was hard on their heels. I did hear my Auntie shouting that Steadman was not with them. I had that dream two or three times a week for a long time and I use to wake-up exhausted.

Question: What is happening when you wake-up but can't move, or that you feel that you have woken and have even got out of bed but you suddenly find that you have not and that you are still in bed. I can remember once that I had even gone downstairs to go into a room and had the door shut on my fingers, it really hurt, but then I found that I was still in bed. I could see my hand on the pillow beside me but I could not move it?

Answer: That's a hard question to answer. (pause) Why do we dream? What is the purpose of dreaming? Ask Baba.

Yoga is softening and feeling.
Afternoon tea with Sensei, 14-3-08.

Question:　The more you look into the process of dreaming, the more questions arise, questions following more questions; it is another place you can get lost in.

Answer:　Of course.

Question:　The other day I asked you if we can control our dreams. You answered no, you can only sit and watch the dream. Did I understand rightly?

Answer:　No. You have no control over your dreams, but you are in them.

Question:　I took the meaning of the words, 'sit and watch' as referring to the witness?

Answer:　Can you witness a dream? When I dream, I am in it. Whatever is happening, I am doing it, whether it is good or bad. If I dream, they are always about my army life. The dreams are clear, my actions are clear, my reasons are clear. My actions create re-actions that are clear. When I awake I am exhausted. The dream of the farmer chasing me went on for years. Consciousness flows out.

Question:　Is Spirit consciousness?

Answer:　(After a pause, then the rising his eyes upwards with a slight smile on his face, he uses his hands to express the words he is trying to find to communicate his answer). The core of you is your soul, consciousness flows from your soul.

Question:　Say the point at the end of my glasses represents my soul. Oh, I don't know what I am trying to say, I don't know what I am talking about. Sensei said, "Go on, sometimes it is best that way". O.K. Consciousness has flown out from that point, say to the size of that dinner plate. It gets mixed in with the mind. At some point within the expansion of my consciousness within the mind there rises a feeling that I have gotten myself lost within myself. Then comes the process, the practice of bringing myself back to myself, in order to expand again, but with the awareness of consciousness.

Find the centre line, move inwards.
Evening class with Sensei. 25-3-08.

Question: When you use the word Spirit do you mean consciousness?

Answer: No. Spirit is Pure Energy.

Question: Is Spirit, Prana (Life-breath, life force, vital energy, the five vital airs)?

Answer: No. Spirit is greater than Prana. Although Prana is all encompassing and Spirit is within Prana, but Spirit is condensed. (Sensei used his hands to help us visualize what words can not tell. He made his right hand into a fist and punched it into the open palm of his left hand with a loud bang to demonstrate his word). Knowledge is within Prana, and everything is within Knowledge. Nothing exists that is not in Knowledge. Everything that has been or will be or is, is in Knowledge. Everything comes from Knowledge. That is why Baba can with a small movement of His hand produce any object that He Wills, knows all languages, all persons, all comings and goings, the past, present and future. He has knowledge at His finger tips. If He needs to know something, He looks to Knowledge and there is the answer, instantaneously. Someone once asked Baba why He does gentle movements with His hand as if writing in air? (You can often see Baba doing this while He is giving darshan, vision of a Holy person). Baba said that He was creating new Universes. Within Knowledge, within the Anahata, (heart centre unstruck sound) in Knowledge was the seed principle of Love. God came out of Love, and out of God came all of creation.

Question: Sorry, but this is a question of what came first. The chicken or the egg type of question. This time it is between Prana and Knowledge?

Answer: The egg is not the chicken. What is the egg? (No sensible answer from me). The egg is the food.

Question: (Again, a simple answer, of course the egg is the food for the chicken. Does this mean, Prana is the food for Knowledge?) But what came first? (Sensei is trying not to laugh but is not succeeding very well. Did he give an answer to the chicken and the egg and I missed it?)

The softer you become, the stronger you become.
Afternoon tea with Sensei, 27-03 08.

Question: When you talk of Spirit, what do you mean? Is Spirit, God?

Answer: In Hinduism, the name Brahman refers to the Primal source and the ultimate goal of all beings: Impersonal Supreme Being. Also in Hinduism they have the Trinity, the same as in Christianity. The Trinity is found in all religion somewhere, it has to be. The Hindu Trinity is called Brahma, the Creator, Vishnu the Preserver and Shiva the Destroyer. In the Christian Trinity the Creator is called the Father, the Preserver is called Son and the Destroyer is called Holy Spirit. Shiva and the Holy Spirit are just different name for The Spirit. The Spirit does Gods work, both the good and the bad. Shiva/ Spirit is the Destroyer of ignorance, and the embodiment of spiritual wisdom.

Question: So when the Holy Spirit descended and entered Jesus' disciples, it could be said that Shiva entered them?

Answer: Yes, (then said with a smile) but only the good part.

Question: So they became self-realized in that moment, enlightened beings. Is this what happens to a person when they become or reach the level of self-realization, The Holy Spirit/Shiva enters them? Is our practice to prepare for this moment? Is Spirit always there, waiting for that moment when we are open enough, surrendered enough to receive the Holy Spirit /Shiva?

Answer: Spirit is always ready. It is us who are not.

Question: What is Prana?

Answer: Prana is all embracing, everything is Prana, (Sensei points to the chair he is sitting on). What changes prana are vibrations. Baba takes a bit of prana in His hand, blows on it, changing the vibration of the prana into an object. If you had the knowledge of vibrations, you too could make anything. Baba is in the centre, the core, the heart of Knowledge. Prana is the vital essence, the motive force.

Question: What is the difference between Atma and soul?

Answer: Atma is the sum total of all beings. Atma is pure Consciousness. (Brahman is identical to Atma; Words I read in a Baba book that night, it seems Sensei's words needed re-enforcing.)

Question: Can the Sahasrara, (crown chakra) only be opened by the descent of Holy Spirit/Shiva, or is it only opened by the ascent of the Kundalini? *Answer.* If God Wills, the Mulahara, (root chakra at base of spine) will be stimulated, this will then stir the Kundalini (potent primal energy that sleeps in the base of the belly) triggering its ascent up the Sushumna (column of energy in the spine) opening the gates of each chakra as it ascends. One of our practices is to breath deep into the belly, taking the inner breath into what I refer to as the cauldron in the pit of the belly, just above where the Kundalini sleeps. The inner breath is pranic—energy. When we breathe out we leave behind as much pranic-energy as we can so that we keep the cauldron topped up with energy ready to overflow into the Kundalini when the time is right. Also on Saturday morning we do the practice of preparing the sushumna for the ascent of the kundalini. We find the centre line (the sushumna within the spine), then we move down the centre line stopping at each chakra for a moment or two till we reach the Muladhara charka, (base of the spine) then we move back up till we reach the Ajna (forehead chakra) This traveling down and up the sushumna helps to prepare the sushumna for the ascent of the kundalini. We practice so that the channel within the sushumna is straight and narrow. That is why I keep saying during the practice, "moving inwards." Jesus said "The path is narrow". The path is the sushumna. If the kundalini ascends in a person who is not prepared for its ascent, the energy from the ascent of the kundalini will be all over the place. The person will not know what has hit them. All their gates will be shut and the energy will just be banging into these gates with force and rebounding all over the place. This happened to someone not that long ago. Baba needed this person awake so He stimulated the root chakra and then sent the person to me. I knew what had happened as soon as I saw the person. I explained what had happened, and then we got to work, doing the practices we do on Saturday mornings, traveling down and up the sushumna and the practice of taking the inner breath into the legs and the other parts of the body, opening all the gates within the body. I did say it would take about a year for the energy from the ascent of the kundalini to completely settle and it has. This person, by the way, is a very old soul. He is being visited by many Great Souls, Saints, Enlightened Beings and Avatars.

Question: Is consciousness always there or is it waiting to come?
Answer: People don't realize how often they are close to receiving. Sometimes consciousness is knocking, but for some reason you don't feel you are quite ready for it. It is us who are not prepared to receive.

Let go.
Afternoon tea with Sensei. 3-4-08.

Question: When I had finished recalling the teachings from last week and putting them down on paper, it seemed to me that the Holy Spirit/Shiva is one and the same with the kundalini. Is there part of the Holy Spirit/Shiva that is within us called, the kundalini? You have said the chakras can only be fully opened by the ascent of the kundalini, but it also seems that the Holy Spirit/Shiva as It descends opens all the chakras. Does the kundalini work with the Holy Spirit? Or are they one and the same? Is it our practice that stirs the inner Holy Spirit/ Kundalini to the knocking of the outer Holy Spirit/ Shiva? Is the kundalini another name for the Holy Spirit/ Shiva within us that lays dormant in the belly, until it is awakened? When you see painting of Jesus' disciples, what usually represents the Holy Spirit is flames of fire coming out of their heads, the flames are not pointing downwards! Ok, who awakens what, why, when and how?

Answer: Have you written that down yet? No, well then, write what you are trying to say down, and I will read it.

Question: Are what you call the gates within the body situated in the same area as the joints of the body?

Answer: No, the gates are all over the body. There are over 72,000, gates. That is why on Saturday morning we practice taking the inner breath into the legs and so forth, then finish by taking the inner breath into the belly and staying there. You can practice taking the inner breath into the belly for 10minutes, or 20 minutes or one hour. When the gates are shut, the energy released by the ascent of the kundalini crashes into these gates, (Sensei uses his right hand to demonstrate. He makes it into a fist and punches it into the palm of his left hand) rebounds and shoots of all over the place. This is a very unpleasant feeling and can cause the body to shake, sometimes violently.

Question: When the gates are all open, do they stay open or do the shut again?

Answer: They stay open and the energy gently flows through the gates, as the wind does a flap.

Softening is the keys.
Evening class with Sensei. 8-4-08.

Question: Have you read the question, yet?

Answer: What Question?

Question: The one about The Holy Spirit/Shiva and the kundalini being the same?

Answer: The kundalini is not the Holy Spirit. The kundalini is dormant energy curled up at the base of the spine. It is pure energy.

Question: You have said that the chakras that are rooted in the sushumna (column of energy within the spine) can only be opened by the ascent of the kundalini.

Answer: Yes, I can see no other way.

Question: But what about the descent of the Holy Spirit?

Answer: The Holy Spirit can, if need, or if ordained or it could be something to do with the person's karma, stimulate the kundalini to rise. It does happen. The practice of keeping the inner-breath within the belly is the practice of collecting the energy, the pranic-energy that you breathe in with the breath. Instead of letting it all escape with the out-going breath, you hold on to as much as you can within the belly, pushing it down mentally further into that space in the belly I call the cauldron, as the rest of the breath flows out of the body. You can do this practice for half an hour, or until the belly fills comfortable within its self. You practice to keep this space, the cauldron topped up until the pranic-energy over flows into the kundalini. The kundalini then begins to uncurl and enters the root chakra (muladhara, base of the spine) and starts it's ascent up the sushumna. The kundalini will only ascend as long as there is pranic-energy flowing into it. The first time the kundalini rose within me, it went as high as the second chakra, (svadhisthana self dwelling place, element; water, concern; ego and sexuality.) then went back down. The kundalini ascent can only be known through experience. The length of time it stays, and how high it rises, is due to the amount of pranic-energy that it has at its disposal. Once the excess prana/energy has been used the kundalini recedes until further prana overflows and stirs its ascent again. *Howard*. Why is the kundalini represented as a serpent?

Answer.   Because of the destruction it can cause. Some do not want Love they only want power. They want only the powers of the lower chakras, then greed takes over and all hell brakes lose. They are not interested in the heart chakra, the Anahata, (the unstruck sound, the centre of compassion). They are not interested in Divine Love. When the Anahata is open, there is no room for greed.

Howard: A Guru told me once, that I needed not bother to focus on the lower chakras, just concentrate on the forehead chakra, (Ajna). Is this right?

Answer: I can not see how it is. The sushumna has to be clear. To keep it clear is the practice we do on Saturday morning. If the sushumna is not clear, straight and narrow, the kundalini energy will flow all over the place. It needs the boundaries of a straight, clear and narrow column of energy, the sushumna, if it is to travel upwards safely, opening each chakra on its way. The only way that I know and the only way I can see of creating a clear channel for the ascent of the kundalini, is the practice. The feeling of our way into the sushumna and finding the centre line, moving inwards as we move down the centre line. Stopping at each chakra for a few moments, as we travel down and up the centre line, many times. This is done to remove any blockages that are within the sushumna. You can not jump up the sushumna that is why I say during the practice, "don't jump". At the end of the practice, we breath in through the medulla, (the centre where God's Breath enters) down into the Anahata, (heart chakra, unstruck sound, seat of Divine Love) and hold the breath there for 10 seconds before we breath out. This will enhance the expansion of the Anahata.

You can stay this way if you wish, I would.
Afternoon tea with Sensei, 10-4-08.

Question: Did you say 72,000 gates within the body?

Answer: Yes.

Question: That is a lot, there can't be much space for anything more?

Answer: The body of light is made up of channels. (Pause) I saw a program on the television the other evening; I think it was last Monday evening. It was a good program for what it was trying to say. It talked about how we have over the ages added to our knowledge. How someone would discover or find out about something and then they would pass this knowledge on to someone else. They might not have got it all right, or it might have been an idea of something in knowledge. They might have just touched upon that knowledge. The person they told could look into that bit of knowledge and may be find out more. This is how, slowly, over centuries, the knowledge of how our world came into being, has grown. It was a good program, but I thought they are missing something fundamental. O.K. If you want something to happen, what do you do? (Here I go again), "You will it to happen," Sensei's face showed that it was not quite the right reply. I jumped in quickly with "You think it". Yes, for anything to come into being, it has to be thought of. We could create a new cloth by putting one yarn and other yarns together, but the yarns we use, had already been thought of, or else they would not have been there for us to have used in our creation. Who thought of all of this into being? Everything is outside, thoughts come in. That is why nobody has ever found or discovered an eighth note or colour, because it is not out there. All the musical sounds and all colours we create or experience come from a mixing of the original seven notes or colours. No eighth note or colour is out there.

Question: When the kundalini recedes, do all the chakras rooted in the sushumna close?

Answer: Yes.

Question: So you have to do all the work again?

Answer: What is needed is all around you (pranic-energy).If you practice earnestly, the practice, will become a habit. The stronger the habit, the deeper it is ingrained in the sub-conscious mind. When the practice is strong, the practices will then continue automaticity, from the sub-conscious mind.

Question: Is it painful when the kundalini ascends for the first time?

Answer: No. If you have done the practice, you are prepared for the ascent of the kundalini. You should be doing the practicing everyday for at least half an hour.

Question: I am now, well since Tuesday evening. I have been sitting every evening for about three quarters of an hour for the last three months, but I have not been doing the practice we do on Saturday morning. Why is that, we know what we want, but we keep putting it of?

Answer: We still want to play with it. We say "I'll practice this evening", then when evening comes, we say, "I will do it tomorrow".

Question: That's like me saying, "But not tonight, I am too tired". But what you said the other evening, brought home the fact that it is up to me, to make sure there is enough energy within me, for when the kundalini (the dormant energy at the base of the spine) starts to stir. So that it can ascend all the way to the top, the sahasrara (crown chakra), opening me up to self-realization, an enlightened soul in this body. God will not do it for me, but He has given me the choice.

Answer: God does sometimes help. But yes, and when you sit and do the practice of keeping the inner-breath in the belly, hold on to the prana that is within the breath. Sieve out the pranic-energy from the bulk, and let the rest leave.

Let go. Let go. Let go.
Afternoon tea with Sensei, 10.4.08

Question: I have been listening to 'Creation' from 'The Hymns from the Vedas'. It is beautiful, all of it. At one part it say's "Out of the centre of OM came Truth." It speaks of High Truth.

Answer: Yes, of course. OM brought with It all of Knowledge. OM is the First Sound that came out of the Love Principle deep within the heart centre (Anahata) of Knowledge

Question: It sings of the order of creation, which is very similar, if not the same, as how scientists now speak of the order of things.

Answer: OM is what scientists refer to as the Big Bang. Within OM came Prana, (energy, the motive force, the vital essence, vitality, vital air, vital breath.) The vibration created by the sound OM, exploded outwards and continues to. The vibration of OM has no limit. It's nature is expansion. The vibration of OM is everywhere; there is no place it is not. God put His thoughts into OM. Prana (vital essence) exploded outwards within OM. Prana is the motive force, the energy, the vital essence within creation. All of creation is made out of Prana. The sun, the moons, the stars, all that you see and all that you don't see is made from Prana and is sustained by prana. (pause) Baba, I feel, will open the Anahata, (heart centre, unstruck sound, seat of compassion).

Question: The Earth's Anahata or the people?

Answer: May be both. My kundalini has gone down, but I have been left with enough knowledge to do my work. I have been kept here, or I would not be sitting here now.

Question: When the kundalini has ascended all the way to the Crown chakra, (Sahasrara, beyond time, space, and elements. Infinite Consciousness) can you still function in the world?

Answer: Of course, look at Paramahansa Yogananda, and his Guru, who was a householder, (had a family) Swami Sri Yukteswar Giri, and Jesus, where God-realized masters. There have been and still are many God-realized masters who have lived or are living in the world, some as householders. Most live a quiet ordinary life and are unknown to the majority.

Question: Is this state of being immersed in the Sahasrara, (*Infinit Consciousness*) also known as the state of Samadhi?

Answer: Yes. (Pause) People don't realize that we are the first generation of humans.

Gather yourself back, into yourself.
Afternoon tea with Sensei. 17.4.08.

Question:: Sensei, can we go back over what you meant, when you said people don't realize that we are the first generation of humans.

Answer: I was not referring to a generation as in ancestors, but a generation in the evolution of mankind. The generation I refer to goes back to when God created mankind and up to, the present day. We are now at the cross-over, so to speak. Mankind's physical form was complete way back then; it was the mind that needed to evolve. Mankind had all the tools he needed within his body, two eyes, a nose and mouth, two hands, two feet, ears, legs, arms, and all the working parts inside. There was no need for the body to change that much, but the mind needed to evolve, for within man God placed His knowledge. The mind was young back then and needed to expand to experience that Knowledge. Now we are at a crossing point, not as individuals, but as the whole. The human race stands at a crossing-over within its evolution. This crossing could take thousands of years for us all to complete. Of course, some have already crossed over. Some have come back to help others. But now the majority of the human race is standing at, or coming very close to crossing-over. When mind started expanding, it runs away with it's self. The further it run the faster it went and the ego ran with it. Now people have started to realize or feel that something inside is teaching them. Slowly but surly people are turning inwards. Although India is the bedrock, it is global. The generation that is coming will have a deeper understanding, will become Christ-like. Their heart chakra, (Anahata, unstruck sound, seat of compassion) will be fully opened. For Jesus did say, "*what I do, so will you do*". It will take time, but it has started. It will come. You have to be aware of at least a bit of Gnostic within you. Everyone has gnosis within them, but they don't feel it. The theologians of all religions have buried gnosis under all their rational analyzing. God/Brahman does not need to be rationalized or analyzed. Brahman/ God needs to be experienced, needs to be felt. Say, a person was reading about the birth of Jesus, they might start to think, how can that be? When a feeling arises from within them, Yes, God could place a baby in a woman's womb. That is gnosis, knowledge from within. They don't know how or why even, but they feel it is true. People do not see that what they are looking for is inside, not outside. I can remember when I was in the army; I started looking for my Teacher, a Guru. I felt that I was ready, that was my thoughts in those days. I was like that. I am ready, where are you? I had a good friend who was a Cockney, (an East Londoner). He would ask, "What are you looking for Taffy?" I told him that the scriptures say that when you are ready, your Teacher/Guru will come. I am ready so where is he! One day, I was laying on my army bed looking up at the white roof of the tent, when I saw a blue spot, on the roof. At first I thought some idiot had painted a blue circle on the inside of the tent's inner roof, we could have all been in trouble for that. Then I became aware that the blue spot was moving. One moment on the roof, the next on the wall. It finally dawned on me that it was my mind that was moving it. I learnt to still the blue spot by my everyday army rifle practice. I would focus on the blue spot, as if I was aiming. I found out later that the blue spot was the bindu, know as the blue pearl.

Question: How old were you then?

Answer: Nineteen, may be eighteen.

Question: I know you don't talk about this part of your work, but please hear me out. I know you have worked on many different levels on the astral worlds, now your kundalini has gone down, does this mean that you are Earth bound now, so to speak?

Answer: Yes, I have been kept here, to teach. The word Sensei means 'one who has been before'. I have been and I have come back.

Question: It must be hard?

Answer: Yes, but interesting.

Moving inwards
Evening class with Sensei. 22.4.08.

Question: Are the chakras completely closed before the ascent of the kundalini?

Answer: No, the chakras are pulsating.

Question: Are people aware that they are dying when they are in the process of dying?

Answer: Yes, most people.

Question: When they have left their body, are they aware of the transition?

Answer: Most people. There was an elderly woman that I knew that had died in hospital. She had crossed over, but then came back. The nurses where comforting her, saying 'its all right now, you will soon be home with your family,' but she replied' I don't want to go home, I want to die. It is beautiful.

Question: What happens when you die? I know it is the body that dies, but what goes with you?

Answer: Everything! It can be liken to a tree shedding a seed. Within the seed is all the knowledge, the blue print of what it will become. How it will grow, what type of tree it will grow into and how tall it will grow. Within the seed will be a map of its branches, the depth of its roots. Its leaves, the shape of its leaves, the colour of its leaves, the number of its leaves. The flowers, the fruits and the seed. So the soul seed within us, when it leaves takes with it the blue print for its next birth. The blue print is made up of all the knowledge you have gathered in this life time. All your actions, good and bad. Your character, your virtues and vices. All the subtlest of feelings and your actions, the thoughts behind the action, the intentions behind the thoughts all help to make up the soul seed's blue print. All this knowledge is added to the knowledge that already exists within the soul seed from previous lifetimes. And like the seed from the tree holds within it the ancient knowledge from all the trees that went before. So does the soul seed hold within it, the Ancient Knowledge.

Question: Can you sometimes try to hard with your practice?

Answer: Yes, trying to hard can sometimes make you tense.

Question: When I am practicing keeping the inner-breath in the belly and I am just sitting, not trying so hard, (as in force) but still focusing on the practice, I feel the inner-breath in the back, (as opposite to front).

Answer: The inner-breath is in the back.

Question: When you leave your body this time, will you choose to come back?

Answer: No, I'll be off like a shot. No, I'll choose to come back, why not.

Soften, all the way through
Evening class with Sensei. 24-4-08.

During a group discussion on what we now refer to as the next generation of humans and how the different aspects of what we call extra-sensory perceptions will become common place. Telepathy came into the discussion. Sensei then spoke about the first time he actually realized that he was telepathic.

Sensei: I was at work and some of my work-mates were playing a game on me. It was a game of passing a message from one person to another without the use of words, but using subtle movements of the hands. While they were passing the message, I realized that I knew what they were communicating to each other. I did not know how, I just knew. The young apprentice, who had started the game, knew I knew and he was a bit put out and said to Phil, the person he was passing the message to, 'You told him!' Phil replied he had not. Then I realized that Phil had told me but, had not known he had. I said to Phil, 'You and I are telepathic'. Phil's reply was that of a typical Welsh working man. So I wrote a sentence down on a piece of paper and asked Phil to say what I had written down. He said it word perfectly. We became a 100% perfect in communicating telepathically with each other, nobody could fault us and many tried. Once as a work gang we were working away and as Phil was the foreman he stayed back at the yard. At the place we were working there was a lot of tools and materials needed. The lads asked me if I could send the list to Phil telepathically so that they will be able to get there quicker. I told them to make the list and I will send it. The list was long and the young apprentice did not believe that I could do this. A bit later the lorry arrived with the things that were needed. Also Phil wrote a note to that young man saying, 'now do you believe?' It is a wonderful way of communicating with another human being; I got much pleasure out of it. Sometimes if Phil and I had not used this skill for a few days, I realized that I could not just do it. I had to put my mind into a certain place in my brain. I had to feel for this place and I found it. I remember speaking with Phil about this, and we both agreed that we must not think when we are going to send messages telepathically to each other. There was a place we needed to go into. I can recall a few others that I realized were telepathic. One was a young girl. A daughter of a woman who still comes to the Dojo. I was at their house one evening and I was telling her grandfather that his granddaughter was telepathic. He would not believe me. So I asked the girl to go into the other room and closed the door behind her. The grandfather had the bible at hand, so I just opened it up and read a few verses. The grandfather was leaning over and following the passage I was silently reading, so he knew what I was sending. The girl recited as I was sending it to her telepathically. She recited the verses word perfectly. The Grandfather was shocked and very frightened. He was visibly shaken. He told me later that it took him a whole week before he felt himself again. Being telepathic was so natural, there was no excitement in it, so to speak and it has nothing to do with being spiritual. Anyone can become telepathic. You don't have to be on a spiritual path for this ability to manifest. But I do feel that if anyone finds that they are telepathic, it will open up the door to Spirit. I no longer use the telepathic way of communicating with people. I enjoyed it in that setting, but things change and we have all gone our different ways. I no longer feel the need. It is like all things, it can help but it is not needed.

Question: I can remember asking you a long time ago whether certain things were needed to reach self-realization, like being a veggie or being able to meditate and back then you said, No, but it helps.

You are not the body, who the heck are you then?
Evening class with Sensei. 13-5-08

Question: There are so many natural disasters happening. In the last 10 years they seen to becoming one after the other, and just lately there has been a typhoon that has struck Burma with winds of 120mph causing floods and taking thousands of lives with it. And then two weeks later there was a massive earth quake in China also taking thousands of lives. Why?

Answer: I can only repeat what Baba has said. He said that one of His main reasons for His coming is, to neutralize man's anger that has gone out of control and is affecting the very atmosphere and penetrating deep into our planet Earth. If He had not come the disasters would be 20 fold worse.

Discussion: Chris came in and also asked Sensei about the disasters that have happened in the last month. This led to a discussion on the forces that are within the Universe. The power of gravity was talked about and how it is so précise and a fundamental part of the Universe. Chris brought up the theories of the black holes within the Universe and how they seem to work. Sensei just said "The black holes are scrap yards."

Get to know yourself.
Afternoon tea with Sensei. 15-5-08.

Question: Is everything that we have experienced consciously or not, stored in the memory?

Answer: Yes.

Question: Where is the memory?

Answer: In the sub-conscious.

Question: What is the sub-conscious?

Answer: A memory library.

Question: Does the memory library hold memories from past lives?

Answer: Yes.

Question: Is there anyway to dispose of the memories, it must be chocker-block by now?

Answer: No.

Question: Is our memory library part of a universal memory?

Answer: No. (Pause) It is hard for scientists to accept that the whole of the Universe, the manifested and the unmanifested, all of creation, came out of One Word that came out of The Mouth of God and with it, all Knowledge. And the Word, the Sound of OM, is still coming out of The Mouth of God. The Universe is still growing, expanding in all directions. Someone once asked Baba what He was doing when it looked like He was writing something in thin air. Baba said He was creating new universes. Baba has also said that mankind within the body as it is now, can not go beyond the home solar-system; it is not built for that. The black-holes, that I call scrap-yards, pulls things in, then breaks the objects down and releases the innate primal energy that was within the objects back into the Universe. The black holes are there to keep the Universe's channels clear. Now it is time for me to go, I don't want to but I have to.

On your own then.
Afternoon tea with Sensei. 20-5-08.

Question: I read in a book of Sai Baba's teachings that consciousness flows within the sushumna.

Answer: Yes, it enters through the medulla.

Question: Is the inner-breath consciousness?

Answer: (pause) It comes from it.

Question: I ask this question because not long ago I spoke with you about feeling the inner-breath as heat in the back of the belly when I did the practice without force. This heat is felt in the area of the sacral and a little above. I wondered if theses two were closely linked or one of the same.

Answer: Good, you are waking it up (kundalini), it's been asleep so to speak. (pause) I was watching a T.V program the other night. It was about a young man who wanted to become a monk. To become a monk in this monastery some where in the Himalayas, he had to first prove that he truly wanted to become a monk. He was told that before he could enter the monastic order, he had to run many miles through the mountains over very rough ground. They filmed him as he ran, and every now and then he would stop to kneel and pray. His prayer was being translated as he prayed. It took me by surprise, it was the same prayer my granny use to pray. They were both praying that their countries would be ruled wisely. They both started with the Ruler of the country, the King or Emperor, next came the governments. They prayed that the people who had power in the country would be honest and upright. They prayed for the teachers, the farmers, the merchants. They prayed for the people of their country.

In the stillness.
Evening class with Sensei. 3.6.08.

Question: I enjoy singing and chanting and sometimes, when my mind is all over the place during the practice of sitting in stillness that is all I do. When this happens, I feel at least I am facing the right direction. When I am chanting and singing I feel heat from my head to just below the heart centre. I feel it enters through the medulla. Out of three Yoga paths, if I had to say what path I was walking, I would say the bhakthi path. Will this take me all the way?

Answer: You are getting there, good. That heat is energy, power. Power entering through the medullar is the greatest power, but you will have to enter the stillness at some point. I can remember when I was young and we were all singing hymns in full voice, from the heart, tears would flow from my eyes. I could not help it, it just happened. First my eyes would fill with water, so much that I could not see out of them, then the water would just over flow. When I was very young I felt embarrassed, but then I thought, 'what the heck'. This does not only happen with spiritual songs, it can happen with ordinary songs. It is the vibration with in the singing of the song that brings the tears of joy. You feel the vibration, you can not think it, and don't stop it. Baba said that people who cry have very very very big hearts. Years ago village people or town people would come together and sing. Not only in the churches or halls, but in the local pubs and neighboring houses. Many years ago coming back from London after a competition, the train we were all on was held up. There were about a thousand of us and we all got out on to the platform to wait. As if on cue, we all started to sing together. It was a big station with many platforms and many people were waiting for the trains to start running again. Everybody just stopped what they were doing to listen to the singing. When the trains started up again nobody wanted to leave. We sang all the way home. People would stop and look in amazement as the train went past. Can you imagine what it must have sounded like? A train with a thousand voices whizing past. A singing train. People have forgotten the joy of singing.

At the Queens Jubilee party 1977, there were over a thousand people. All had come together to celebrate and sing. We sang non—stop into the early hours of the morning. We had to make our own music back then and making our own music has been taken away from us, has been stolen from us.

Question: Going back to the subconscious and memory. You said that everything is stored in the sub-conscious. The subconscious is one big memory bank. All our past lives are held within the sub-conscious mind and all that is to come will be held within the sub-conscious. Have I understood correctly?

Answer: Yes.

Question: How far back in our sub-conscious mind, do the memories of our past lives go? Do they include animal lives?

Answer: Sensei looks down at the floor as if to say, 'don't forget insects'.

Question: Does it go all the way back?

Answer: (pause) I don't see why not. Some of us were still with God when it began. We followed behind, saw what was happening. That's in the sub-conscious.

Question: When someone becomes self-realized, I have heard that they see all their past lives. As they are so centered in the Self, they see this without judgment and therefore do not judge others. When this viewing of past lives happens, is the person within the sub-conscious? Does it come from the sub-conscious?

Answer: The sub-conscious mind evokes or awakens the memories of past lives. The everyday mind will only register what has made an impression on it, but the sub-conscious recalls all that is happening around you and within you. I can remember being at someone's house and we where sitting down watching television, when the little girl said "my mummy wears dresses like that". Her mother said that she had not got dresses like that. The little girl replied, "My other mummy." Her mother ran out of the room. You see, the little girl's mind was still open. There was a man who was very interested in these children who could recall past lives. He went around the world researching these stories and listing them. By the time he visited this little girl her mind had closed. She was twelve when it happened, but in some it stays open. Buddha was self-taught and went back into Spirit. He went inwards, into the mind. We are putting too much on Baba (*God*). Buddha said *"you are the ones that are causing the problem"*. Buddha came upon the inner-teacher and realized that the inner-teacher was in everyone. Buddha lightened the vibrations of the world. Everyone has gnosis within them, but it needs to be touched for it to quicken. You could be reading about the birth of Jesus. Your logic starts to tell you that it is not possible for a virgin to give birth, but a feeling arises from somewhere deep inside and somehow you know that it is possible. God can create life within a virgin. That is Gnostic. Someone else might start to read the Bible but soon put it down saying it is a load of rubbish. But another person could be reading it and as they read, they say to themselves, "I can do that" or "I have felt that". They might not even truly understand what it is they have done or felt but they know it is right. That is Gnostic.

Slow deep breathing in the belly.
Afternoon tea with Sensei. 5-6-08.

Question: What is behind the sub-conscious?

Answer: Behind the sub-conscious is (Sensei spreads out his arms) Consciousness.

Question: About being enlightened and seeing all your past lives, what is it like? Do you feel them or do you experience them?

Answer: For me, it was like watching dreams go by. My eyes were closed and I just sat and watched.

A good habit is softening.
Afternoon tea with Sensei. 12.6.08.

Question: After listening to your teachings on the mind. It seems to me that the practice is a tool that enables us to move beyond the everyday mind, into the sub-conscious. Then through the sub-conscious into consciousness. Is my understanding correct?

Answer: Yes.

Question: Is it correct to say, that the everyday mind is tiny compared
              to the sub-conscious mind, which is tiny compared to
              consciousness?

Answer: Yes.

Question: What is beyond consciousness?

Answer: Consciousness is everything.

Question: Is Atma and Consciousness the same?

Answer: Yes and no. In India, there are many words relating to the
              same thing. On the other hand, one word could have many
              meanings. There are many different languages spoken in India
              and what could mean one thing in one place could refer to
              something else in another place. Baba has a habit of explain
              something very beautifully and simply. Then He will say, '*but
              you could say it like this*' or ,*ike that*', which can cause confusion.
              When there are many words meaning the same thing, it can get
              confusing. Baba has a bad. (Sensei stops, looks up with a smile)
              Yes, it is a bad habit of doing that.

Question: I have been reading a book on Shirdi Baba. Sai Baba is a
              reincarnation of Shirdi Baba. I can't quite understand how this
              is. I know it is true but I don't understand how. You have said
              that Sai Baba is an incarnation of God in His fullness, a Proona
              Avatar, and that Shirdi was an Avatar but not a Proona Avatar.
              How can this be? Sai Baba is Shirdi Baba. Sai has declared
              this.

Answer: The Soul that we know now as Sai Baba was the Soul in Shirdi
              Baba. When God incarnated in the Soul of Shirdi Baba, He did
              not bring all His powers with Him. He did not need them all.
              When God incarnated again in that Soul which is now known
              as Sai Baba, He brought all the powers with Him, for He needs
              them all, in this part of His Mission.

Question: Was Jesus an Avatar? Did God incarnate in the Soul of Jesus,
              but not in His fullness.

Answer: Jesus was a Realized Soul, although, He had to go and learn
              from others who He was, for Him to become a Christ. Jesus
              declared this when He said, "*God and I are one*". He also
              declared, "*What I can do, so can you*". He did not mean that we
              can become like Him straight away!

Question: You have said that Jesus was the reincarnation of Elisha and that John the Baptist was Elijah. Jesus' disciples must have been reincarnations of great souls to have been so close to Jesus?

Answer: Yes, of course.

Question: Also Mary Magdalene. She was a great disciple of Jesus, and Mother Mary who gave birth to Jesus. They too must have been great souls.

Answer: Yes, although nowadays some people are trying to find evidence that Jesus married Mary Magdalene. If He had, His descendants would be able to trace a line back to Him. Nobody can trace an ancestral line back to Jesus. There is no line that can be traced back to Jesus.

Question: Going back to past lives, I can recall, and so can others, that you once said you could remember being a crocodile and that you enjoyed being a crocodile. Also when I asked (not long ago) if you were with Jesus, you said 'yes'. I know you don't talk about past lives, and I also know I am just being inquisitive, (Sensei looks to the heavens as if to say, 'here we go again'.) but were you with Shirdi Baba?

Answer: Yes.

Question: Also, Mike mentioned the other day, that he had explained to a woman that the only difference between them was that his Sahasrara (thousand-petaled chakra at the crown of the head. Beyond time, space, and elements. Infinite consciousness) was open and her's was not as yet. He also said that he was with Krishna, and as he always refers to you as The Master, were you with Krishna as well?

Answer: Yes.

Question: Thank you. Some years back, you where talking to a group of us and you said that every night when we go to bed, when we start to drift of to sleep, we are actual moving into meditation. During that process of drifting of to sleep there is a point when we actual fall into sleep, but if we had carried on in that state, just before sleep, we would move into meditation. Have I remembered correctly?

Answer: Yes, and I can remember once, when I was at that point in full awareness, I thought, shall I or shall I not. Then quickly thought, what the heck, why not, and fell into sleep.

Bring all of yourself back to yourself.
Evening classes with Sensei. 17-06-08.

Question: Where is the Universal mind?

Answer: The Universal mind is the Field of Knowledge.

Question: Is there a demarcation line between the separate states of mind or do they flow in and out of each other? Like there seems to be a line around the sky, where the sky finishes and space begins but in truth there is not.

Answer: They flow.

Question: The other day you referred to God as The Soul of Shirdi Baba and Sai Baba.

Answer: Yes, when God incarnates it is The Soul that incarnates.

Question: We are part of God. God is within us.

Answer: We are all part of The Soul that we call God.

Question: Some time ago, in answer to a question you said that the baby is three to four months old before the soul has fully entered it. Does The Soul of God fully enter the newly formed baby? Is all of The Soul within Baba?

Answer: Yes. God/Atma/The Soul, (there is only One but the wise call it by many names.) is smaller than the smallest and bigger than the biggest. We are unable to understand this with the mind. It is beyond the comprehension of the mind, but you can feel it. Not straight away, but it will come. Maybe at first, as a gentle feeling of just knowing this is true. This feeling is taking you inwards, opening the door so to speak, while you wait patiently for an experience of this Truth in its fullness. It is the natural state of Being.

Howard: My son told me the other day, that the teaching they are receiving, tell that the soul that was in Gautama, was on Earth eons before he was born as Gautama, who became The Buddha, founder of Buddhism and back then He was also fully Enlightened. Have you heard of this?

Answer: No. Why do they say that and why have we not been told before. If this is true, it will have a profound affect on all religions.

Howard: Would the soul of Jesus appear now in the form that we know? I mean if He comes now from wherever He is, would He appear as He was 2,000 years ago or would He have a different form.

Answer: He is the same and will always be the same.

Howard: What about Baba.

Answer: No, Baba is all forms. (Pause) I feel that when Baba wills that the heart charka of humanity to open, 95% of the people will accept His will. We might not realize at this moment that this is what we are searching for, but we will. Baba has said that it will manifest more deeply in the next generation.

Howard: What are the differences between the Akashic Records and the Book of Life?

Answer: The Book of Life is a personal record; the Akasha Records is a field of energy that stores all events of creation however small.

Chris: A friend of mine had a ring materialized by a Guru who is over on a visit. As he was materializing the ring she said his eyes where turned up into his head and that she could only see the whites of his eyes. Something I have seen happen many times with you. Was he really manifesting the ring or was he transporting it from somewhere else?

Answer: His eyes were turn upwards into his head because he was grabbing hold of consciousness. He needed consciousness to create. Creation comes out of consciousness.

Question: Hey, you once replied when I asked about your eyes disappearing into your head, "that they needed to go somewhere".

Answer: (A little chuckle) Dorothy once asked why my eyes kept changing their colour. I told her it was the energy and that I could not help it.

Question: Nothing can be added to us and nothing can be taken away, because within us, the essence of us is God. We came from God, a spark of Divinity. Our soul is a part of The Soul. Is this our truth?

Answer: Yes, but how far back can we remember, can we comprehend, can we grasp, can we feel? May be I can grasp what 2000 years represents, but what about the billions of years before that. How many billions of years did it take for the Earth to form, and then how many more, before the first crawly things crept over the Earth. The souls that were within those crawly things are the same souls that are in us. Souls evolve, forms change, but like the seed of a tree, the soul holds within it the blue print of what it is, what it will become, one day. Why did I come to It, through the martial arts? The martial arts taught me more about Jesus, than all the church sermons, the Sunday school classes, and Bible study groups that I attended during my childhood and my youth put together. Why? Because through the teachings of the martial arts, I could understand what Jesus was saying, I could feel it. I could be reading from the Bible and come across a passage, I would stop reading as I realized that, I can do that, or, that is what I am doing. Jesus said, "What I can do, you can do". My teacher was a Japanese Master who taught me Judo. I can remember standing in line with my Cockney mate from the Army when the Master came up to us and asked us if we were Christians. We knew we were most probably the only Christians there, but we said "Yes". He said, "Good, read the Bible, it teaches what you will be practicing, 'out of the belly of man living waters flow'. You are practicing to do this". The Japanese master referred to the belly as the Hara, and the energy that flows around the body like a system of rivers and canals, Ki. The brain that is in the head is just a storage bank. In the belly/hara is the second mind/brain. Second as in, it has to be developed. When we are full of negative and impure emotions like anger and greed, the Ki can and does intensify these emotions. Ki can intensify your anger or enhance your compassion, the choice is yours. Ki is pure energy; it is the thoughts that create good or bad. Through the practice, we are slowly letting go of these harmful negative emotions, allowing the Ki to heighten the vibration within us. Compassion overflows from the Heart centre, (Anahata, unstruck sound, element: air, concern: intuition and compassion) into the Hara/ belly. The Solar plexus centre, (Manipura chakra, site of gems, element: fire, concern: mental) is the outlet for that energy. Ki is that energy. The more Ki, the more power.

Question: What is the soul?

Answer: Energy. It is your own personalized energy.

Question: Did the soul brake away from The Soul, or was it sent away?

Answer: It was given a gentle push. (Sensei demonstrated this gentleness by using his foot).

Phil: Last week we talked about how some music can give us a deep and wonderful feeling of joy, so deep and so wonderful that it can bring tears of joy to our eyes. It seems to me that the old hymns has this ability more than the new ones. Hymns like The Old Rugged Cross, to mention one.

Answer: Yes, the people who wrote them put their heart and soul into the hymn.

Phil: I was also talking with someone the other day about how there has not been a new opera written for a long time. Is this because there are no more people left that can compose operas from their heart and soul?

Answer: Is it because of the lack of people or that there are no more operas in the heavens?

Be still.
Afternoon tea with Sensei. 19-06-08.

Question: Which of all the religions speak closer to the Truth or explain the Truth clearest?

Answer: In my opinion, Hindu is the closer religion.

Question: Why are the words *Be Still and know that I am God,* feel so powerful to me. I love those words, they go deep and I feel them as they enter the very marrow of my bones.

Answer: Those words are very, very powerful. So powerful, but they are not taught in the sermons or the Sunday schools. I can not remember listening to a sermon on those words. They are not studied in the Bible classes or at the Christian collages, or they would be taught. So great is their power. Theologian just pass them by because they don't understand them, they don't feel their power.

Feel the stillness.
Evening classes with Sensei. 21.06.08.

Howard: Sensei, last Saturday during Meditation I went into the hara. I was looking downwards and saw a tiny hole, like a pin head. I said to myself, "well, the breath is not going to be able to get through that!" Then the breath came, sounding like a tornado as it rushes in, swirling and filling the whole of the hara, before it slipped through the pin-hole. When I looked into this pinhead hole I could see it lead into a pipe like channel. Can you clarify this for me?

Answer: (Sensei was gently laughing quietly to himself as He listened to Howard) Yes, I was watching what was going on, and yes, that was the entrance of the sushumma. As Jesus put it so well, *"It is easier for a camel to pass through an eye of a needle, than a rich man to enter the Kingdom of Heaven."* The eye of the needle is the pinhole you saw. The pipe is the sushumma. The Kingdom of Heaven is the Crown chakra, (Saharara, thousand petaled chakra, beyond space and elements, Infinite Consciousness). The breath takes you in. I can remember being in line at a dojo in Korea, when the Master told us to read The Bible, John chapter 7 v38. He quoted *"streams of life-giving water will flow from the belly"* He then told us that this is what we will be practicing. Do you know, I had read that passage many times before and it did not mean anything to me until then. You have to be Gnostic, or at least a little bit. Theologians read the Bible but do not grasp the deeper meanings of Jesus' teachings. The story of the camel and the eye of the needle were understood on one level but they don't go deep enough into words, they do not go within themselves. To understand gnosis (knowledge of spiritual mysteries), you have to go in.

Howard: How does the knowledge that we have gathered in one lifetime, come through into our next?

Answer: The soul brings it back. The subconscious is in the soul. Think of the seeds of a tree, say an oak tree. The oak tree will shed many seeds, but they will not grow into identical trees. Some will grow branches this way, and some will grow them that way. Their roots will go different ways. It will also depend on the environment they are place in, but they will all grow, when the conditions are right, into oak trees. For the oak tree is within the seed.

Question: Is the subconscious in the soul?

Answer: The subconscious is everywhere.

Chris: It is all over the place, I say this because my mind was everywhere during Saturday's meditation, except on the centre line. On the most trifle of things Sensei.

Answer: Sometimes we need that to happen to know. I can remember once sitting with Stuart in the Dojo, we where waiting for someone else, so we where just drifting on the outskirts of meditation. While in that space of moving into meditation, I came to an edge of what I would call a chasm and as I look down into the chasm I knew that sleep was down there. I had a choice, I could jump the chasm and go into mediation, or I could fall into the chasm and go to sleep. I open my eyes to have a peep, and Stuart seemed to be looking at me with an expression of, well then Sensei, what are you going to do? I thought what the heck and went to sleep. Sleep was a bit of a mystery to me when I was younger, one minute I was awake, the next it was morning. That seeing, the chasm of sleep, only happened to me that once.

Howard: Where are we when we are asleep?

Answer: Outside the body. (A soft smile comes to Sensei's face) The first time I actually experienced being out of my body was when I was thirteen. I was laying on my bed with my hand behind my head looking out of the opened window. When suddenly I was outside the window, I wondered where I was, so I looked around and found that I was in the air. The very next thought was, "if Auntie comes in and shuts the window how will I get back in?" I did that sprint in less than a second, that is the truth.

Howard: Do you have to move into the sushumna (column of energy within the spine, the pipe Howard saw.) and ascend to the Ajna (forehead chakra) to meditate?

Answer: No, you can take yourself into a condition, a space. The first stages of meditation are the same as the stages of going to sleep. Many times while I am taking a yoga class, during the softening, (a gentle meditation in letting go) there are snores coming from all over the dojo. They all start the softening very well, too well maybe, for they fall into sleep. But for higher states of meditation, (samadhi, state of super consciousness resulting in union with or absorption in the ultimate reality, the Atma) you ascend through the sushumna

Don't think so much.
Afternoon tea with Sensei. 26.06.08.

Question: I have re-written that last part about Ki.

Answer: Ki is a mystery.

Question: I have a book at home on Shiatsu, I looked up Ki in there hoping that it would give me a definition of Ki in a few words. After looking through the book, I thought that I might take an introduction course on the subject.

Answer: Good.

Question: Can I bring the book for you to look at, so that you can let me know if it is a good book for me to read on Shiatsu?

Answer: Yes. When I was young, everybody thought I had magical hands, because back then, when you started to practice the martial arts, you had to know how to put your partner back together, before you took him apart. Shiatsu was part of the teachings within martial art, but is not now.

Question: Is that because when the martial art came to the West, the people who brought it over did not think that the healing part of the art, had any importance to the actual teachings of the physical aspect of martial art. They just wanted to teach the oriental art of fighting?

Answer: No, the Japanese Masters who brought it over, taught the art of healing before they taught the art of fighting to their students. What is the good of learning how to fight before you have learnt how to heal. But as the martial arts moved into the area of Sport, many things were left behind. New rules were made to govern a sport called martial arts. They would come and tell you that you can't do that; you need fully trained people in First Aid to deal with that sort of thing. The first time I used Shiatsu outside martial art was at home. I was in my bedroom laying on the bed when I heard a lot of noise and confusion outside on the landing. I went out to see what was happening, and there was my Granny, my two Aunties making a lot of noise and crowding around the bedroom door opposite. I pushed them out of the way and when I could see into the bedroom, there was my nephew laying on the bed with plugs up his nostrils. The sheet was covered in blood. I pushed everyone out of the room, including the doctor. I went in and lifted a foot and placed it on a back of a chair so that the whole leg was elevated. I gathered the kokyu (energy) in the hand, then hit the sole of the foot three times with the hand (Sensei illustrated his word by hitting the palm of his right hand on to the palm of the left hand that represented the foot. He did this with a firm and rhythmical movement leaving a short pause in between each slap). It was like turning off a tap, but nobody asked me what I did or how I did it. Once while judging a Judo competition one of the competitors got cramp in both legs, from the hips down to the feet. A crowd of people were around him, but no one could help him, it was thought that he would have to drop out of the competition. I went over to see what was happening. I had to push the crowd away. When I could see what had happened I picked up each leg in turn, I did what was needed to be done and the cramp was gone. The person finished the competition and won. Again nobody asked me what I had done. Once a Doctor came to the Dojo and he brought a young man who could hardly walk. He was bent over and needed help. I got him to lay down on the mat and worked the points on either side of the spine in the small of the back. The Doctor was leaning over my shoulder watching. He asked me what I was doing, I am not sure if I said Zen shiatsu or Oha shiatsu. The doctor told me later, that if he was young man again, he would still study to become a Doctor, but he would also study these other arts of healing. (Sensei lifted up his thumbs to show how the tops of them leaned backwards from the top joint, with a comment that at one time, they where at right angles)

Question: I thought it was the top of the thumb that you used?

Answer: No. There was a young girl who suffered from asthma, I was round their house when she was having a very bad attack, the asthma pump was not helping, nothing was helping her. I went and put my palm of my hand flat on the centre of her chest, and as she breathed in I pushed in and when she breathed out I released the pressure. The asthma attack went. (Sensei again used his hands to demonstrate the movements he used and again they where rhythmical and focused) Her mother was a nurse; she asked me what I was doing. I showed her what to do and she has past it on to many other people. There was another young man who had damaged his back. The doctors had tried many different treatments to cure his back, but none worked. He had been in back straps for a long time. He came to the Dojo with his wife. Again I got him to lay on the mat and worked the small of the back on each side of the spine. When he got up, his back was pain free. As he walked out of the Dojo he gave his straps to his wife. I did wonder whether the back was healed for good. So I went round to his house the next morning. As I knocked on his door I was not sure what I would find, but when he opened the door he was standing straight and he told me that his back was fine and that he was not wearing the straps.

Question: Can souls journey together? I mean, when souls reincarnate are they attracted to souls they have been with in past lives. Say a mother and a son in a past life could reincarnate as friends in a future life. When people form strong links with each other in a lifetime, are those links carried forward into other lives?

Answer: Well yes it can happen like that, but it is more to do with what you do! what you are attracted to! that will have a greater affect on your next life. *Question*: Like I am attracted to Yoga?

Answer: Yes (with laughter in his voice) may be next time you will be born a Hindu and live in Puttaparthi.

Question: Only if you are there. Sensei, have I been with you in past lives?

Answer: You could have been, it does happen like that.

You will never get yoga by thinking.
Evening class with Sensei. 1-07-08.

Question: Is Ki, Prana?
Answer: No. Prana is everything; (pause) Ki is mental Spirit.
Question: By mental Spirit, do you mean that you mentally draw the Spirit into you?
Answer: Yes, but it is hard to find words for Ki.
Question: You said the other day that Ki is magical.
Answer: It is.

Question: How do I stop letting things pull me out? I blame outside things but I know it is my reaction that pulls me away from myself.

Answer: Practice and energy.

Question: I was going to say that I seem to have no energy. I get tired easily in any sort of confrontation situations, but then; more practice will give me more energy.

Answer: You are practicing?

Question: Yes, but maybe not enough.

Answer: Let us understand what vibrations are. If you act in a negative manner to something that you feel is negative, you add to that negative vibration. Somebody might have triggered it, but you went out with your reaction, to the negativity. Accept people as they are.

Deeper softness.
Evening classes with Sensei. 15-7-08.

Howard: Is not the breath a very important part of our practice and if it is, why did you tell me the other week, to leave the breath behind?

Answer: Did I? (Pause) The breath is a very important part of our practices, it takes you in. The work we do on Saturday morning, includes taking the inner breath to different parts of the body. We do this practice to prepare the body to be able to receive higher vibrations of energy, without harm to the body. The practice of keeping the inner breath in the belly is in preparation for the ascent. What I call the cauldron is like the first bucket. When that is full to over flowing with inner breath, the overflow of inner breath will enter into the second bucket. From this bucket, the inner breath causes a light pressure that stirs, or aggravates the primal energy (kundalini) that has been laying dormant, deep within the belly. It has been curled up asleep, so to speak. But, as the inner breath starts to aggravate it, it starts to uncurl, and if there is enough inner breath to keep up this aggravation, the primal dormant energy (kundalini) will start its ascent up the sushumma, (column of energy in the spine) When you have practiced regularly for sometime and have become acustom to the feel of the inner breath, the sub-conscious will take over the practice for you, allowing your conscious mind to go further inwards. The practice of following the breath, takes you inwards, until one day, the sub-conscious naturally takes over. For the sub-conscious knows what you want to do, due to the continuous practice. In time experiences will become your teacher.

Howard: Why did I see that? (Ref to pg70, 24/6)

Answer: Why not? The first thing I saw was my dinner. I was a young man then. I had eaten my dinner about half an hour before I sat to meditate. I went inwards and looked down and saw my dinner. It was a surprise, but I knew these things happen. You need to understand that you were inside! you were in your inner mind, using your inner eye. It is different for everyone.

Howard: Why is it so different?

Answer: Vibrations are different. Jesus put it so wonderfully when He said "Be Still!" And when He spoke about the camel and the eye of the needle, (Matthew, ch 19 v 23), and the road being long and narrow (Mathew, ch7 v13&14). He was speaking about the sushumna and how hard it is to get in. The sub-conscious knows, the new mind (the mind of a baby) did not know. The new mind needs to turn inward at one point.

Howard: Should I dwell on the energy in the coccyx?

Answer: Yes. The vibration in the coccyx wants to unwind. Remember, the road is narrow, keep it clean, practice. More tests will come! It will seem as if everything is trying to pull you away from your practice, from your meditation.

Howard: Negative energies?

Answer: No, not negative energy, more like people and worldly things pulling at you, pulling you away, back out, when you what to go in! You might have just gone up to sit in meditation, or practice with the inner breath, when the door bells go. You get up to answer the door and there is one of your friends. You invite him in; make him a cup of tea, then sit and chat. You could have said, come in, make yourself a cup of tea, I'm sorry but I am busy at this moment, I'll be down in about half an hour.

Howard: Does the kundalini go up and down?

Answer: Yes but it can stay up.

Question: I thought that it stays up?

Answer: Let's get it going up and down first. (Pause) The sub-conscious gives free-flow to breath. Yogananda, (Parahansa Yogananda, God-realized master, 1893-1952) was exhausted the first time the kundalini ascended. Keep the rhythm going, keep the inner-breath. The inner-breath does the work. You have two breaths. First breath is the out breath; you go *in* on this breath. The second breath, the in breath, you stay *in*. The inner-breath will accumulate till it overflows, aggravating the kundalini, which in turn, causes the kundalini to ascend.

Howard: Are you the breath?

Answer: No. You are inside, using the inner-mind, and the inner-eye. You draw the breath in! You are not outside taking the breath in through your nose, (Sensei illustrated this, so we could understand the difference between breathing in, and drawing in).

Howard: You can go in at anytime?

Answer: Yes, but you will also be able to do that one day. Think from the belly. Part of you is in there now. At first it is like hit or miss, but then sub-conscious realizes, "oh, this is what you want". Then you hit it. Develop the hara, feel from the belly. When in control, the sub-conscious takes over; it's too much for the head.

Howard: In this book it talks about the physical heart having an affect on the spiritual heart. Is this correct?

Answer: Nothing physical can touch the astral body. The life-force, the soul, fills the body. There is no part of the body that is not full of life-force.

Question: I thought the soul was in the heart chakra?

Answer: The soul is everywhere.

Question: Then why do we meditate on the heart centre?

Answer: Because the heart chakra, (Anahata unstruck sound, seat of compassion) is the seat of Divine Love. You draw the soul back in into the heart chakra, (Anahata, unstruck sound). (Sensei is reaching above his head, out to the sides, in front, below, in fact anywhere he could, so that we could understand that the soul is everywhere and we need to pull it back in.) The kundalini needs to rise, the soul has to rise. Even Yogananda had to wait.

Many times when he was a young man he asked his Guru to grant him enlightenment, but he was told, not yet, you are not ready, be patient. Carry on doing the Saturday morning practices, everyday, not like this one. Breath is the first step. God did not make it difficult, we make it difficult.

(Howard to Chris: "Talking about babaji, (an ancient, but still-living Master in the Himalayas) is it in Yogananda's book that there is a list of Masters that started from babaji, and that one of them was Sensei's Master". "Yes" says Chris.)

Only in the stillness will you hear the Voice of God
Afternoon tea with Sensei. 17-7-08.

Question: On Tuesday evening you said the soul is everywhere in the body. I thought the soul resides in the Heart chakra, (Anahata, unstruck sound). On the way home I was pondering over this, when I recalled that Baba's also has said that the soul is everywhere but if you want to think of the soul in a place, say as for meditation, think of the soul in the Heart chakra, (Anahata). Why are we told to meditate on the Heart chakra?

Answer: The soul is everywhere, inside and outside. The Anahata (heart chakra, unstruck sound, seat of compassion) is where Unconditional Love comes from. It is the seat of creation. The soul is everywhere; you need to draw it back into the Anahata (heart chakra)

Question: The soul is everywhere?

Answer: Yes.

Question: Consciousness is everywhere?

Answer: Yes.

Question: (I just looked at Sensei.)

Answer: You gather the soul and you gather the consciousness. When they come together that is enlightenment, and that is something else.

Yoga Starts
in the Belly.

Yoga Starts in the Belly.

Experiences.

My first experience was of the bindu (a chakra and although it is inside you, it appears outside. It is called the blue pearl). I was laying on my bed in an army tent in India, when I saw a blue spot on the inner tent ceiling. At first I thought someone had painted this blue spot on the ceiling, but then in started moving. One minute it was there, the next on a wall of the tent. It was up and down, all over the place. It moved very fast in a zig zag movement. Then bang, I suddenly realized that the blue spot was not outside of me, but inside. Then I wondered why it was moving, which brought me to the realization that it was because of my mind. My mind was moving. That was my introduction to the movements of the mind. Then I started a practise on controlling the mind. I had no one to show me a practise. My Japanese Master was in Korea and although I would visit him now and then, it was more for reinforcement and confirmation. So I made my own practise up. I trained my mind by using the everyday army bayonet practise, which uses a hanging ring, just big enough for the bayonet that was attached to the rifle to go through into the padding behind the ring. So, for the training of my mind I used my thumb and first finger to make a circle, which represented the hanging ring which I placed just in front of the centre of my forehead, and I kept the blue spot in that circle made by my finger and my thumb. If it moved out of that circle, I brought it back. I would sit for a long time everyday practising. My army mates would come in and ask me what I was looking at. How could I tell them, they could not see it. In the end they would just say "there he goes again". When I could keep the blue spot firmly within the circle made by my thumb and first finger, I started to slowly move my thumb and finger away. In the beginning, the blue spot would follow the thumb and the finger as I moved them away. My mind was moving. But with practise and patience, in the end I could keep the blue spot firmly in the centre of my forehead. This showed me how deep I had gone into my mind.

Although I had not been practising before I went to India, I always wanted to know. Like in the Bible I would read passages and I wanted to know want they really meant. Somehow I knew there was more in the words that I read; more in the teachings of Jesus I was taught. I would read a passage in the New Testament; say the passage that said Jesus told one of His disciples, "To you I give the key to the Kingdom of heaven." I wanted to know what the key was and nobody could tell me. I know now, it is softening. When I came back from India my family and friends thought I was crazy. Although later on one or two of them would ask me sensible questions. I was always practising, it became natural to practise. I would be walking along the road and a family member or a friend would call out to me, but I would be in practise and not answer. Some thought I was being stand offish. I can remember once walking by the bus station and one of my Aunties was at the bus stop with a friend. She called to me; I did a full cartwheel then shouted good-bye and walked on in practise. The Bible is full of sign posts, even though many have been taken out, but they are there if you look. All movement comes from stillness, learn to move in stillness.

I remember one evening I was sitting in a chair in the backroom of the house in meditation, when I felt something inside. I started to move from the chair to go into seiza (a meditation position that is taught in the Martial arts), but as my knees hit the floor, instantaneously, bang, all was blue (blue pearl). I could see nothing but blue, and I lost all sense of direction within it. The feeling and the colour of the blue was so beautiful and so dense! It had all come from inside. It took me a long time to get to my bedroom. I had to feel my way with my hands. First along the long passage way to the front door, then feeling for the stairs, I started my way up with only the sense of feeling to help me. It is lucky my bedroom door had a different knob to the other doors, so I knew it by its feel. When I got into my bedroom, as soon as I laid on the bed I went to sleep. When I awoke in the morning, I was back as I should be.

There was that time when I built the Walls of Jericho. I was at work and the work's lorry was just about to go off on a job. For some reason, no. it was more an inner-feeling, I decided to build the Walls of Jericho around it. I had never done this before, and I don't even think I had thought of it before. My mates in the lorry asked me what I was doing, they where use to me by then. I told them I was building the Walls of Jericho. I walked round the lorry seven times, and then went off to measurer up a job. When I came back, the lorry had not moved and my mates were still in the lorry. I did not know then that I could build the Walls of Jericho, I was practicing. I then had to unbuild the Wall of Jericho by reversing what I had done. There are many stories and many times I had to find out how I was doing these things. Remember I was practising on my own. I had no physical teacher to ask. My teacher was the inner-teacher, myself. But there came a time when I had to let it all go, I knew I had to, for the feeling to let go came from inside. It was a lovely kind of energy to work with. I still have so to speak, one foot in it, no, it is more like I am walking along side it. It is experiences that give you knowledge, even little experiences. Now I have to go.

* (Swami Muktananda said: that the vision of the 'blue pearl' bindu is itself the Truth, and only one who has had this vision has realized the Truth.)

Hard to teach.

Yoga is hard to teach, it goes beyond word. You learn yoga by feeling and by experiences. You ask about the bindu. How can I put this into word? I could tell you it is a chakra, and the chakra is inside of you but it appears as if it is outside. But it is more than that, and how ever much I can tell you, it will always be more. I can tell you that you can't search for it, for it comes as if by it's self. It is like a by product of your higher consciousness rising. You do not have to work to create a bindu; it is all ready there within you and when you have seen it, have experienced it, have felt it, you know how far you have travelled inwards. You can not really teach these things, you can only point the way. They have to be experienced! And our experiences will be different, due to our vibrations. You can only teach the basics, take our Saturday morning practise. I can only say things like "keep the centre line", "don't jump" or "move inwards", but the experience you have is due to your vibration. Someone many feel more in one chakra, and someone else something completely different. Our vibrations also changes due to the condition we are in. That's why Jesus said "be still". Learn to move in that stillness.

Yes, yoga has a few stretching exercises that you can teach others that help to soften the physical body. As you stretch, you let go of the breath and you soften natural. You soften on the outgoing breath. With practise you will stay in the softness, you will not go out on the incoming breath, but go deeper with the next outgoing breath. Softening helps you into the stillness and you will learn to do the exercises in that stillness, not straight away! It all depends on you. Softening is walking backwards into yourself, but it is more than that. As I said before, you can't teach Yoga, you can only encourage. Yoga is taught from the inside. People tell me what they are experiencing due to their practise. I say good, carry on, go deeper. They are, so to speak, revving up inside. There is no limit to the softening, there is no limit to the deepness, and there is no limit in becoming. The experiences have to be different due to our vibrations, but the goal is the same. We need to develop inner-discipline, for it is our weakness for other things, which stop us moving inwards. Consciousness is within and it is beyond words. It is a feeling. Consciousness brings awareness of everything else, it teaches the mind to feel and see. More consciousness creates more awareness. This is very important. We are looking somewhere else, but within the core of us is God, Eternity. We have to unite ourselves with what is already inside. We separated ourselves from our Self.

Walking backwards into yourself.

Death is beautiful, for you are going back into yourself. Most old people know when they are going to die. They are prepared for death, they start to let go, they move inwards naturally. Anyone who has accepted their death will naturally start to move inwards. If death is accepted, dying is a process of walking backwards into yourself. If death comes through an accident it could be confusing to start with, as there had been no time to prepare for death, to accept it. The spirit of the person might not have realized that death had accorded, but it will settle and go back into itself.

The Holy Spirit.

The Holy Spirit is God's Work Horse and it can be liked to the super charger of a car. The mind is like a magnet to the Holy Spirit, for it helps draw the Holy Spirit into you. You could say that the Holy Spirit's job is to aid the soul to become Christlike, It grants fruition to the soul. As Jesus said, "What I can do, you can do". Our practise is to prepare for the uniting of our spirit with the Holy Spirit. It is the feelings from the soul and the everyday feelings that create our spirit. The feelings that emanates from our spirit can pull down the Holy Spirit, and the touch of the Holy Spirit can awaken our spirit. The Holy Spirit is outside of us and we pull it in by our hwyl (Welsh word meaning; fullness, full of happiness, full of life, good humour) The Holy Spirit is the likeness of God and God's Will comes through the Holy Spirit, but it works both ways, the Holy Spirit comes through God. The Holy Spirit is the Gnostic Spirit, and It is something we earn the right to. The Holy Spirit gives to us, but it gives us what we need, not what we want. We become more aware of the Holy Spirit as we become more gnostic, and when we become Christlike, we will experience the Holy Spirit in fullness. Your everyday spirit is very close to your will; it is in harmony with your will, but separate. It pushes you to do things; it gives you the power to go on. The everyday spirit has highs and lows and it feels, but it is not Gnostic. First we need to teach the mind to feel. As I have said many times before, we feel our way inwards, we can't think our way in. Then Gnostic knowledge, knowledge from the Holy Spirit, will start to flow into you, this will naturally lead to a deeper awareness, as you open up to consciousness. The more you open up to consciousness, the more you draw the Holy Spirit into you. The soul is life, but within it, is the spark of Divinity. There are degrees in the spark of Divinity, due to actions or non actions of past lives. For the spark to build up, it has to have input and output. The required inputs and outputs come with experiences. Because of these experiences, the Holy Spirit gives Itself more and more to us. There is no end to the expansion of the spark of Divinity. Slowly, by experiences we earn the right to *become*. Our being (soul) has to reach a certain level of being to *become*. Jesus in his life as Elisha became a Kriya Yogi. In his life as Jesus he became a Christ. There is no limit to becoming.

India.

One of the army camps I was based in while in India, was next to a village called Ranchi. This army camp was bigger than all of Llanelli put together, and my tent was in a far corner next to a wall. On the other side of the wall was a very wide river, but it was dry with only a little stream in the middle that you could step over. I use to sit on this wall watching the people from the ashram that was also on the other side of the wall, practicing their yoga. At first I just watched, and then as I got braver. I put one leg up on the wall, then over the wall. Then a thought came, I can do that and I started to copy them. The swami who was teaching the yoga was watching me and beckoned me down with a wave of his hand. I went down to meet him, and the yoga that he taught me back then, I still teach today. I was with that swami for about six may be eight weeks. I don't know if that ashram was Paramahansa Yogananda's ashram. I did not ask, for I did not know of Yogananda, I was a very young man back then, all of eighteen years old. Where the army camp ended, the jungle began. It was like what you see in a movie. Just inside the jungle was an old temple, and the jungle was growing all over it with creepers coming out of it's windows. The swami told me that the temple had died because it had no spirit. He also said that the religions will go back to the old ways of teaching. People will come together in small groups to share, to worship, to experience, to re-discover the inner path to God.

Another army camp I was based at was close to Sai Baba's ashram, and I heard many people talk about Sai Baba. They where saying that He is God come in human form, and I believed it, no questioning. I felt its Truth. Sai Baba was also a young man back then, in fact I am a little bit older. I tried many times to go and see Him, but every time I made arrangements to go, the army sent me off to somewhere else. India opened me to yoga and meditation, to the inner-path that I had walked before. The Japanese Master in Korea helped me to set things more permanently within, and Jesus deepened it. I remember the Japanese Master asking Harry and me if we where Christians. We told him we where, he then said "Good, read John chapter 7 verse 38, as the scripture says, Whoever believes in me, streams of life-giving water will pour out from his belly: This is what you are practicing to do." I learnt more about Jesus and His teaching during my stay in India, than I had leant from all the sermons, bible study groups and Sunday school classes that I had attended in Wales. The church leaders could not give me answers to my questions. I can remember being in Kashmir, and sitting inside an open café by the side of the road having a cup of tea and there was a magazine on one of the other tables. I went and picked it up and as I opened it at the centre pages, there was a big photo of the family who were the custodians of the tomb of Saint Isa, Jesus the Christ, in a place called Srinagar, Kashmir. This family have been looking after Jesus' shrine, since Jesus' body was placed in it. The responsibility had been past down from father to son since that time, and the Indian government gave the family sole rights of custodianship in the 17th century. This took me by surprise and I ask the Indian who was making the tea if he had heard of this. He said "Yes, Jesus tomb is just down the road." Just down the road was about 200 miles. This again I felt was true, but I could kick myself now, because I left the magazine there at that roadside café. I did not think I was young. When I went back a few days later, it had gone. Then there was the time I saw the image of Bombay Harbour in the sky, as clear as if I was looking at it, and it was not only me, the rest of the platoon saw it to. We where travelling through the jungle at the time, and we decided to go down into the ravine to get some shade and be cooler. We all put down our packs and leaned back into the side of the ravine, which naturally took our eyes upwards to an opening within the roof of the jungle, and there in the sky was Bombay Harbour. Nobody at first said what they where seeing. Each thought they may be hallucinating, but soon we where all just looking in amazement, we could see the ships moving. When we got back to Bombay, we found that it had been in all the newspapers. It was a natural phenomenal; the last time it happened was in the 1800's, but we were a thousand miles away! While I was in India I spent all of my spare time in meditation or in practise, and of course this flowed into my not so spare time. It became natural to me. Harry, my mate, got so use to me he would just say to others, "oh leave him alone, Taf is just doing his thing". Then one day I started searching, I started looking for someone. Harry noticed this and asked me who I was looking for. I told him I was looking for my teacher; for the scriptures say when you are ready your teacher will come. I felt I was ready, so where was my teacher. That was my thoughts back then, I was young. After I had been searching for sometime, out of the blue, it suddenly came to me. I started laughing; Harry said "what are you laughing at Taf." I told him that the teacher I was looking for was inside of me. Harry just looked at me and walked on.

Softening is the Key.

Softening is the key to the Kingdom of Heaven. When I was young, I used to read the Bible and wonder about what was actually being said, in the pages of this Holy book. I would ask questions, but I got no answers. The answers started to come when I was a young man. Many of my questions where to do with Jesus' teachings. I can clearly remember wondering and asking, what did Jesus mean when He said "to you, I give the key to the

Kingdom of Heaven"? What was that key? The answer came when I was a young man and the answer was softening. All the practises we do, we could not do with out softening, we can not go into meditation without softening. Softening is walking backwards into yourself. As we grew up, we walked away from ourself, now we have started to walk backwards to ourself. We could not enter the stillness, without softening. Softening is the key. Jesus said "I go to prepare a place for you", He was saying, I will guild you to a higher level of consciousness. He also said "that the road is narrow" and "if thy eye be single, thy body will be full of Light". The road he was referring to is the sushumna, (column of energy with in the spine) and the single eye is within the forehead centre, (ajna chakra, also know as the third eye). When this chakra/eye is open, the body is full of light. The highest level we can rise to while within a human body is Christhood, but this is not possible without the softening. You can not learn about God from outside, you have to go inside. To move inwards you soften. Baba has said "that people are developing meditations that are to difficult". It is practise we need, not more complicated ways. Keep the practice simple, but stay with the practise. Soften and move inward, that is all, the rest will follow. Whatever Gnostic teachings that are left in the Bible, there is still enough to let you know you are on the path. When you soften you are teaching the mind to feel itself. When the mind feels, you find inner sign-post; this is good, for you will know you are on the way. Feeling comes with softening. I am a guide; I give you hints or pointers, but let you find out for yourself. For then you will know! And no one can bluff you anymore.

The path more important

When I came back from India, I already had one foot firmly in and I was trying hard to get the other in. But there was no one I could talk to or discuses things with. No one around me had ever heard of yoga, let alone practised it. If I had told them what I was doing and what was happening within me, they would have put me in St David's hospital. If I had told them about Sai Baba, they would have thrown away the key. So I just carried on with my practise. Every day I practised, some part of me was always in practise. People in the end, just accepted that I had a few strange ways about me. The swami in India, when I told him about the blue spot (bindu), said that he was surprised that I had experienced it. Yogis have sat in practise for years to reach the level were the bindu reveals itself. I had only just started the practise of yoga and I had only known the swami for a few weeks, when it happened. As I have said before, I was just going to bed. I was actually holding up the blanket and had just put one leg under the blanket; the other was still on the floor, when the bindu appeared on the inner roof of the tent. It was not long after that, that the army sent me somewhere else. All told I spent about six weeks with the swami, but we kept in touch with each other on an inner level, until he died a few years later. When I was in India with the swami, I realized that some of the yoga practises I was learning were the same or near enough the same, as some of the practises I was learning from my Japanese Master. The martial arts also teach the spiritual inner journey of man. More so then, than now. The spiritual grounding within the martial arts, are being more and more left out of it's teachings. I learnt more about the teachings of Jesus through the martial arts, than I ever did through the church. The martial arts are built round the hara, (belly). Yoga is built round the breath. The breath centre is in the belly. Yoga starts in the belly. During that time when swami kept in touch with me on an inner level, not only did he give me wonderful information, he let me know that I was going the right way. That was a great help, especially when I was back home. The reassurance was needed, for I was young, and questions were answered.

You could say I was self taught, for I was on my own. I had to find out how I was doing things, and why things were happen. I can remember when I started seeing the energy coming from the chairs and the walls. Every where I looked, the energy was flowing and the colours of the energy were changing and moving into each other, like swirls. Animals can see this. I would watch this little dog watch the energy. I also found out, that somehow I was influencing this energy that was all around. How was I doing this? You Know, sometimes silly things would happen. What I mean by silly things, is that I was shown things when I least expected them, out of the blue so to speak, and in odd and ordinary ways. It was like this powerful energy, was also a playful energy. Or was it me being playful? There are many a time when I laugh till I cried over the happenings. I low was I doing these things? It might have been me or the energy being playful, but I was also serious and the energy is powerful. I would go inwards and the mind would move into the stillness, with out effort. There I would sit until I understood what I was being shown. My teachings came from inside. There are many funny stories of me playing with the energy, but I had to stop. Something inside was telling me, no, I don't want that, the path is more important. When the bindu exploded, it filled me, but I never saw it again. Everything you need is inside of you. You have all the tools you need to find God. God is inside. Not just inside you, but in everything. There is no where that the God is not.

Jesus learnt to become Christ on Earth.

We are learning to become Christ-like. Christ consciousness is within us, but we need experiences to turn our everyday mind inwards. This experience is an inner experience, although it can be triggered by an outside experience. This experience need not be earth shattering, but it turns the mind inwards. A mind turning inwards creates a feeling within. That feeling is the first small step on the inner-path to Christ consciousness. Jesus said the road is narrow, he also said follow me and I will show you the kingdom of heaven. Jesus was teaching the inner-path to God. Everyone has within them this inner-path to God, Christ-consciousness /self-realization. Once you have had that first experience, the inner-pull will always be there, it may be very faint at first, but it will come.

To feel that inner-pull, or to recognize it, the soul needs to be born into a human body. For a human being has that innate ability to wonder and reason, and a yearning to know. From our first becoming, we have travelled through lifetimes upon lifetimes, gathering experiences through outward looking. This outward looking is never ending until we feel that inner-pull. As I have said before, we separated ourselves from our Self. The inner journey is a journey back to our Self.

Jesus also said who so ever believes in me, streams of life-giving water will pour out of his belly. The life-giving water is the primal energy that is laying dormant at the base of the spine. In yoga this energy is called the kundalini. When this energy/life-giving water (kundaline)is stirred, agitated, or awakened you could say, it will move into the sushumna (the column of energy within the spine), which Jesus referred to as a narrow path. The energy/life-giving water (kundaline) will travel up the sushumna/narrow path, opening the six chakras that are rooted in the sushumna/path till it reaches the seventh charka which is above the sushumna, the crown chakra, known as the sahasrara in yoga. This holds within it, infinite consciousness, heaven and is beyond time and space. As Jesus said, the kingdom of heaven is within you. He also said if your eye be single, your body will be full of light. He was referring to the sixth chakra; also know as the third eye, the inner eye. It is called ajna in yoga. When the ajna chakra is open, the body is full of light. When you experience this opening into the kingdom of heaven, this beatitude, no words can describe it, for it is beyond words, but you know and that knowing is all you need.

To agitate or awaken the life-giving water, known as the kundalini (super charged energy at the base of the spine) in yoga, to pour out of the belly, we practise taking the breath deep into the lower part of the belly, into the breath centre. We then keep hold of the inner-breath, (life-force, know as pranic energy in yoga) that has entered on the breath, storing it in what I refer to as the cauldron (breath centre). When there is enough inner-breath within the cauldron, (breath centre in the lower belly) it will over flow and agitate the life-giving water (kundaline) and provide the force that is needed for the life-giving water (kundalini) to flow upwards, up the sushumna, (a column of energy within the spine). But remember, Jesus said that it is easier for a camel to pass through an eye of the needle than a rich man to pass through the gate to the kingdom of heaven. If you are still outward looking, looking to what is yours and what you want, instead of looking inwards to what you are, you will be like the rich man Jesus talked about, and the eye of the needle is the opening into the sushumna, what Jesus called, the straight and narrow path.

This is why you often hear me say, yoga starts in the belly. Deep breathing in the belly brings calmness, a stillness that leaves no room for fear and enough energy for the inner journey. The journey that Jesus taught, a journey that has been taught down through the ages and is still being taught, and will always be taught for those, as Jesus said, who have ears to hear, and eyes to see.

Wonderful stories.

We can read many wonderful stories on the inner-path and listen to many preachers and teachers talking about the inner-path, the path to God. But when we have finished reading the story or the discourse has come to the end, we are the same as what we where before we read the book, or heard the teaching on the inner-path to God and self-realization. However beautiful, however inspiring, these stories and teachings are, we still don't know. How can we know about the inner-path before we have at least touched upon it? The wonderful stories and great teachings are sign-posts for the inner-journey. These sign post are there to let us know that we are going the right way. They give us confidence, but we need to have at least one foot on the inner—path to be able to see the sign posts. Teachings come from within. The inner-teacher gives us the experiences to know, not just believe. The inner-journey starts with belief, but leads to knowing. Even those feelings called beliefs, come from within. Feeling come from inside, thoughts come from outside. To know you have to be inside.

When I was a boy, I was not satisfied in just listening or reading the teachings of the Bible, more so Jesus' teachings than the Old Testament. I wanted to know what Jesus meant, what he was saying. When I heard that Jesus had given to one of his disciples, the key to the kingdom of heaven, I wanted to know what the key was. It bugged me, it would not leave me alone, I wanted to know, but no one could tell me. Looking back, I feel it was that key that started it; it put me on the inner-path before I knew it. Why was I put in that army camp with my tent in the furthest corner and right next to that ashram? The army camp was bigger than the whole of Llanelli put together. The swami/teacher of the ashram would teach me many things, but most did not make any sense to me at first. It was not until I had my own experiences that I understood and knew what the swami had been saying. He gave me sign posts, for the inner-journey. When I first met swami things started moving, answers started coming. It could be likened to a long inwards winding row of dominoes set up on their ends. He gave the first a little flick and the rest followed and fell into place. Of course, we bring with us at birth, all that is to do with the soul. There is a story about a man who was trying to brake up a rock. He was hitting this rock with a big sledge hammer. Sweat was poring off him, his muscles were straining, and he was using all his might. He had just hit the rock twenty times when he put down the sledge hammer to mop his brow. Another man came along and picked up the sledge hammer. On his second hit, the rock broke into pieces. This does not mean that the second man broke the rock in two hits; the rock had been hit twenty times before by the other man. Some people, who have been practising hard for most of their life, may feel that they have not moved very far along the inner-path. Then someone comes along, who they think has only just started on the inner-journey, but is soon leaping and bounding far ahead of them, and they ask why? The answer is simple. The person, who is bounding along with such ease, can be likened to the second man who broke the rock in two hits. He already had twenty hits stored up in his sub-conscious from previous lifes that he had brought with him. I feel that there are many people all over the world at the same level as I am, stimulating people. There is no limit to consciousness, the more we go in the more we expand. It is all there waiting for us; just keep doing what you are doing. The heart can feel the knowing before the experience of knowing comes, why? Because part of us is still outward looking for answers, still looking for God outside of ourselves. God is inside, find Him there, and you find Him everywhere.

The crossing point.

I could have gone to Sai Baba's ashram in India many times, but I didn't, why? Because I know Baba is within me. God is in me, so why do I need to travel half way round the world to be with Him? God is everywhere; there is nowhere that God is not. We all need to truly understand this, God is within us. We are a fragment of God. That fragment is deep within the soul, it is know as the atma in yoga. The human race is now ready to evolve into the next generation. The human race as a whole has come to a crossing so to speak, and it has taken a long long time for us to reach this point, why? Because we needed time to move beyond those animal instincts that we brought with us, the outward looking instincts, to the innate wonder, the reasoning faculties, and the yearning to know, that emanates for the soul. It is only in human form that the soul can turn inwards. It is said that God planted His Knowledge into mankind. That Knowledge was the knowledge of the inner-path. Remember, there has never been a time when we were not. Of course many have gone before us; they are our sign-posts, our teachers, and some of us are now in the process of crossing over. But the majority of us are gathering ourselves together, getting ready for the crossing; even if some of us are dragging our feet. Of course some will not want to let go, that is their choice. During the pioneer human stage, we slowly moved from being an animal-man to a human, and the humanness evolved within us. We have now reached the point of becoming humanly-divine. The choice is ours, but I feel that most of us will choose the path that takes us to the divinity that is within us and has always been within us.

Consciousness emanates from the soul. It is our consciousness, which has been evolving through the passage of time. It has been growing and expanding outwards, but it did not know. For to know is within. Our consciousness needs to turn inwards, all of it, to know, but this is hard. It is only in the stillness that we can control our consciousness, and the stillness is inside, not outside. When we are softening, we are gentle drawing our consciousness in and there will come a point, when everything is still for a moment, in that moment the consciousness turns inward, for it will feel the pull of the soul, it's source of being. Animal consciousness is outside, although when an animal is close to a human, the comradeship that is formed between the animal and the human will pull the animal's consciousness inward. Animals are more aware of what is going on outside, their sense are more alert, more clear. They can see the more subtle elements of life, and they sense the shifts of energy and vibrational patterns quicker than most humans, why? because we have deadened our senses. Human consciousness should be inside. There are different degrees in humanness due to how much consciousness is outside, and how much is inside. So put a hundred percent inside, and enter into Christhood. God is me, always come back to this. God and I are One. To realize this, we have to follow the path that Jesus taught, the inner-path, the ancient path. It is hard to explain, all I can say is that you need to go in, to expand in fullness. To expand without being within, is to get lost.

What is Knowledge?

Out of the Knowledge came God, but God is beyond Knowledge. Knowledge had no direction until God emerged out of the Love principle in Knowledge. The Love principle was in God before the beginning of creation, which the scientists have put at 13.7 billion years ago, and the Earth at 4.5 billion years old. But how can we comprehend even one billion years ago? I can just about comprehend 2,000 years. Knowledge is so far back that man can not give it a figure. We are beginning to understand God, but not Knowledge. We have given God a figure, but people can't understand how Knowledge got there, and don't ask me, for I don't know. It just Is. Scientists try to give figures to the age of the Universe and to the different solar systems and planets, but it does not mean anything. The mind can't recognize that length of time, that distance. We can't comprehend what one billion is, let alone 20 billion plus. It means nothing to us, it is just a figure to debate over, even argue over. And what is a light year other than many billions of years put together. If we can not comprehend a billion miles, what chance have we got with light years? The Ancient Sages had already worked out a way of measuring these sorts of distances and times, it is called kalpa, (1 kalpa = 8,640,000,000 earth years). All we are doing now is proving that they are correct or not. We are not adding to it. All of creation is held within Knowledge, all that is, was and will be, is within Knowledge, and only God can create from Knowledge and only from what is already within Knowledge. Why did God create only seven musical notes? Because that is all there was, there was no eighth note for God to bring into creation. Human beings can not add to creation. The seven colours are already there for the painter to mix. The seven sounds are there for the musician and the five elements for the scientist. There are nine numbers for the mathematician, and all wisdom for the seeker. But what we draw to us from the Creation and how we use it, is our choice. What we draw to us can change the soul's pattern of evolution. Only God can draw from the Field of Knowledge and He gives to man when man is ready. But so long as you know that you are enlightened, you can make use of Knowledge. If you don't know, you can't. The Love principle within Knowledge never created, until God emerged from the Love principle. It's like God was asleep or dormant within the Love principle, until He felt a stirring within. God was, is, and will always be within the Love principle in the Field of Knowledge. But God had to come out, so to speak, for creation to become. You could say that it is the God part of the Love principle that creates and destroys, but they are not separate, they are One. As Baba says, "God is Love and Love is God and nothing happens without My Will".

Imagination is a God given gift to the human race. Everyone has imagination to some degree, and the more we use it the stronger it becomes. Imagination is putting separate things together that are already there. God imagined the world into existence, from the Field of Knowledge. Imagination can be likened to a gardener gathering seeds. Imagination is in between thought and becoming, and it selects from the thoughts that are already there, to create. It is a creative power, but it can only create from creation. So use your imagination wisely, for as you think, so you become, and don't let fear creep into it. Only God can create from the Field of Knowledge. We use the imagination for our inner journey, and the imagination uses the sign posts (seed thoughts) that are already there. Thoughts are brought together and that is your imagination. Everything is already there for the inner-journey, the journey of the soul. You could say the Holy Spirit puts your own unique inner-path together and uses the imagination for you to recognize the sign posts along the way. Imagination can not imagine what is not there, but it can help by enhancing the inner sign-posts. These sign posts (seed thoughts) give you confidence, and confidence gives you strength to carry on, and it draws what is needed for the next step on your inner-journey. No two inner-journeys are exactly the same, but the destination is the same for one and all. This is hard to put into words, for there is too much on the outside to understand, unless we get inside. Remember, you are not the body.

You could liken a new born baby to an empty vase. The substance for the everyday mind is inside, but empty. We are receivers, and we play about with the information that we receive. We develop the everyday mind with thoughts and information from outside, and all too soon the mind is crammed full of this and that. This is why I say mind comes in. Our sub-conscious stores all the information and thoughts that we have received, from past lives, as well as this life. If I wanted to know something that happened five years ago, I have to travel back five years into my sub-conscious. It is the lack of this ability to go back, that stops us from moving inwards to expand outwards. This going back is not to bringing forward, it is just going back. Where I lived as a young boy, I could see four fields from my back door. Let's say the smallest field was the size of three football fields, and the biggest was the size of fifteen football fields. Now think of the size of one football field and imagine being able to count every blade of grass within that football field. Now take the understanding, that every blade of grass within one football field represents a thought within the Field of Knowledge, which is on the Palm of God's Hand. To comprehend how many football size fields are on the Palm of God's Hand is beyond our imagination.

Karma.

Not everything that happens in a person's life is due to past karma, the cause could have happened yesterday, and something's are just due to our own silliness. And remember karma does not only bring the bad, it also brings good. Karma works both ways and it is an ongoing thing that started with our first birth within a human body. We were never meant to be bad, but we where given free will and we made wrong choices, and those choices seems to have gotten out of hand. Also karma does not have to be big; it is usually very small and passes with just a whisper. Karma just flows through our lives. What causes karma are deliberate actions and, deliberate thoughts. For God listens to the mind, not the voice. We work off our karma while on Earth, for the level we go to up there, is fought out down here. We cannot take on each others karma. Only a Master, and not all Masters, can soften or take on the karma for others, and then only if it is for the highest good. Jesus' coming to Earth had nothing to do with karma and He also brought with Him certain powers that He had been given when He was Elisha. When Jesus was fourteen, He was found giving sermons to the priests and rabbis of the temple. That knowledge that came from Him then, He had acquired in His life as Elisha. There had been many great teachers and masters before Jesus, but their lives where not so dynamic. Even though they also performed miracles and had powers over the elements. Jesus' life on the other hand was dynamic enough for something to happen, so that the people would not forget, and we haven't. All the great yogis and masters have great respect for Jesus, for He kept to His path even though He knew from the beginning how it would end. Jesus came to lift humanity to a higher level of consciousness and to do that, He took some of the negative karma of the world and placed it in His physical body. This was a deliberate act of compassion. Jesus first said that He was a messenger of God. Then later on He proclaimed He was the Son of God, and at the end He said, God and I are One. Now the Father has come.

Trying to comprehend the ways or laws of karma is like trying to comprehend the source of creation, it is beyond the everyday mind. Karma is for the evolution of the individual soul, not the body. The karma of all souls is called world karma. Baba is taking on world karma, taking on the negative vibrations that have built up over the centuries, that is why His body is as it is. One day Baba will do something about the world's karma He holds within His form, He will blast it to smithereens. As I have said before, only great masters can take on the karma of others and there are very few in the world that can. It is also always a deliberate act, after taking all into consideration; the master takes on the karma of another soul. We usually play out our karma within relationships with other people, or add to it, good or bad. You could say that the karma of each soul within a family is intermingling to help each other work out their personal negative karma and building up good karma, we hope. Collective karma of any group is the deliberate individual thoughts and actions that have come together. World karma is the sum total of all deliberate thoughts and actions. We as individuals can help lighten world karma by our own deliberate thoughts and actions, or darken the karma of the world. The choice is ours, but by lightening it *we* come together. Sometime ago I knew a man called John, he was a deacon within the church. His story of how he became a disciple of a great master is wonderful, although most of his family disowned him. He was very favoured by this great master, I can't remember the master's name, so don't ask me. The master asked that John be there when he visited London for the first time. Hundreds were waiting to greet him at Heathrow airport. When he came into the departure area he walked straight to John and put his arms around him. During the master's stay in London there were some people asking the master to heal their friend. The master said yes, soon. After a few weeks he took John to the house where the young friend was. He told everyone to leave the room but told John to stay. John told me that he was at the side of the bed, and the master was at the foot of the bed. The master started to chant softly. John was given physic sight. He said that he could actually see the cancer leaving the body of the woman and entering the master. He could see the body coming back naturally. When this was completed, John said that the master turned around and gave the most frightening shout and obliterated the karmic diseases. But remember that not all disease is karma as in pay back time; it could be to do with something we have eaten or just silliness. There are so many ways the body can become ill. We all have the ability within us to heal ourselves and the potential to become healers, but remember all healing comes from God, and there are different levels of healing. What we call spiritual healing can not fail, but karma can only be taken on by a great master. If healers were to take on other people's karma they would all be dead. Eileen has been giving healing here for the last ten years everyday and she is still very much alive. Healing is a deliberate act of the healer. The more pure the intent, the more healing. The healer usually brings down the healing energy into the heart centre then it is released through the hand, although some healers can store the healing energy within their body. Absent healing works the same way as telepathy, but don't ask me how it works. Do not worry about karma or debate over what it is; do not try to make it fit. Use your energy to move inwards and all will become clearer. Learn to feel, not think so much. Be still. Karma is a gift from God that leads you back into your self.

As I said before, healing is a deliberate act of a healer and the person who is being healed; they are both deliberate beneficial acts, from good intentions. As it is a deliberate act it will create karma, but good karma. It will not exchange karma or take on some of the other person's karma. Of course if a disease is infectious the healer could catch it. The healer could also pick up the negative vibrations of a disease or disorder, but that is not taking on karma. A good healer should know how to clear negative vibrations with positive vibrations; many healers have their own little rituals to cleanse themselves. If you think of a disease as something laying on top of a part of the body, the healing energy will sort of push it's way in between the disease and the part of the body that the disease was laying on, making a pathway. This helps to slows down the growth of the disease and gives the body time, space and energy to heal itself. If the healing is for a breakage of the body, the healing energy helps speed up the body's own healing process. Healing works in many ways and on all levels, but your karma is your karma, good or bad. Work with it, go through it, but don't fall into it. When I was a young man I was taught how to heal through the martial arts. The Japanese Masters would first teach their students how to put a person back together, before they taught them how to take them apart. For some reason, the art of healing is no longer taught in most martial art classes in the West. When I was healing, you could say it was a combination of what I was taught in the Martial arts and spiritual healing. There was a time when I was a young man when everyone at work seemed to be suffering from what we called a frozen shoulder. I had to heal them or no work would get done, and even today when some of them see me, they will shout over and say, "Look Di, I can still move it" and they show me how well their shoulder still works. But not all people where happy with me giving healing. There was once this old grandmother. Our work gang was given a job to do at the house where this grandmother lived with her daughter. When we first saw her she was so bent and folded up that we could not believe it, and she had been like that for the past fifteen years. She could only drink her tea though a straw; she could not lift up her head or open her hands. The boys said "Go on Di, you can heal her." Her granddaughter shouted at me and said "don't you touch my granny; I'll have the police on you!" The old woman was sitting in front of me and I looked at her, after a bit I thought, what the heck lets have a go. It was like magic, her body just opened up. Her hand coming up for her to drink a cup of tea without the straw, for the first time in over fifteen years. The Granddaughter was so angry with me; she said she will get the police on to me, but I had not touched her grandmother. Her husband who was a doctor said "you can't be going around doing things like that". I also remember being told by a father, whose boy came to the Judo classes held here, that while they were watching a rugby practise, one of the rugby players got kicked in the side of his face. That kick had ripped opened the lower part of his face on the right side, and no one could stop the bleeding from the wound He said his son kept telling him that he could help, and that he had been shown how to at Judo. In the end the father went over to the group that was standing around this rugby player and said "my son says he can help." They called the boy over and the boy put is hand above the wound and they all watched the rugby player's face knit back together. There are many good healers within this dojo, in both the yoga and the martial art classes.

As for karma, if you do not want to accumulate karma, even the good karma, the best way is to work for the sake of the work, not for the gain from the working. To give for the sake of the giving, to play for the sake of playing, to help for the sake of helping, to do your practise for the sake of the practise. Let go.

Yoga starts in the belly.

Pranic energy enters through our skin, as well as on the breath, although, with most of us it is a very low amount, but to those who know, they can draw it in through every pore of the skin. But remember the air that we breathe in is full of pranic energy (life-force), and all we need to do is hold on to it, not let it leave on the out going breath. Pranic energy is everywhere, like the air, but more. Pranic energy is the energy of creation. There is nowhere in this entire Universe that pranic energy does not fill. Pranic energy is more than life-force; it is the force within the very substance of life, as we know it. Also, as we are breathing, the breath draws goodness or badness into us. The goodness or badness that enters on the breath are thoughts. Thoughts are everywhere; they are in the air that we breathe. We can't get away from thoughts, but there comes a time when we are more aware of the subtle vibrations of thoughts. In advance stages we become in harmony with the breath, then no bad, evil or negative thoughts can settle within us. As Jesus said "Only by thy breath shall I know thee". You could say the good and bad thoughts are fighting for your companionship. As we progress, in time we will be able to suppress bad thoughts, or the feelings from bad thoughts. As Jesus said "get behind me Satan". Satan was a thought! While Jesus was in the wilderness for forty days and nights, all the bad and evil thoughts were fighting for His companionship. Even the Holy are surround by bad and evil thoughts while on the Earth, but they can suppress them, giving them no room within. Breath has a powerful affect on how we think, and as Baba says "As you think so you become". Shallow breathing has not got the strength to keep out negative vibrations and to deal with bad and evil thoughts. Say we breathe in an evil thought. If we are aware of that evil thought, we would suppress it, give it no room. We fight it. If we are not aware of that evil thought entering us, we give it room, and could act on it. Although with some people the action comes straight away. If we practise breathing from the breath centre in the lower part of the belly (cauldron), our breath will become stronger. For we are drawing in more pranic-energy, which helps keep the store house in the lower part of the belly full. Therefore we are less likely to feel drained, to become weak to the forces of negativity. Also the mind becomes quieter, for we have taken our awareness away from the every-day mind and the thoughts that fill it, to the breath centre. This allows our awareness to expand beyond the everyday mind to a heightened state of clarity. This practise of slow deep breathing in the belly will become a habit, if it is practised regularly with patience and given time. A good habit, that takes us back to the innate rhythm of the breath. That rhythm (although innate) was set in motion at our birth, usually by a mid-wife holding us upside down and giving us a slap. If you take time to watch a baby or a very small child, you will see that they are naturally breathing from the breath centre in the lower belly, but all too soon they are pulled out. Breathing from the breath centre gives us the strength to fight the devil (bad and evil thoughts and negative vibrations) and move forward on the inner-path. That is why I say, yoga starts in the belly.

While we are building-up our inner-strength, it is best to keep away from places that tend to hold on to negative vibrations, and people come to that. This of course can be very difficult, but at least be aware of where you are and stay only when needed. When we have built up enough inner strength, we enter a state where the belly is full. A state where there is no room for fear. The belly is calm. And in that state of fearlessness we can move into areas of dense negative and evil vibrations and help lighten them. All thoughts and vibrations go straight to the belly, when belly is full, no negative vibrations can get in. All good or bad vibrational thoughts enter the belly first before travelling up to the brain. If it is a negative or evil vibration it can create hell, when it gets there.

Jesus too had to fight for self-realization, or it would have just slipped away. The negative vibrations and evil thoughts were fighting for His mind. They were always trying to find out what He wanted and then offer it to Him, tempting Him, trying to win Him over, coaxing Him to let them in. But He stuck with His path, even when the negativity and evil vibrations nailed Him to the cross. He was still full and His compassion flowed without distinction, it just flowed and still is flowing. Baba has a very big soft spot for Jesus. Come to that, those negative vibrations and evil thoughts are still trying to tempt the Holy, even Baba.

The mantra OM (sound of creation, the Breath of God, the Word of God.), starts in the belly. The fuller the belly, the more powerful is the vibration within the chanting of the mantra OM. If the belly is full, the force within the vibrational sound of OM will send it to the four corners of the world and beyond. This is not only true for the sound of OM; all chanting, all prayers and all mantras can be very powerful, they draw you inwards, as they expand outwards. Chanting, prayers and mantras should start in the belly, not in the head. You feel a yearning in the belly. That yearning comes from the heart, but is felt in the belly. The sound of creation, OM, is everywhere; it is where we get our knowledge from. There is no place that the vibration sound of OM is not. It is the sound of creation. If there is no OM, there is no creation. The vibrational sound of OM is the very substance of creation, and pranic energy is the force within OM. God's First Breath was the outgoing sound of creation, the vibrational sound of OM. And that First Breath is still coming from the Mouth of God. When our belly is full of prana, and the mind is still, and the yearning is great, when we chant the mantra OM, we can feel the Breath of God within us. But to hear the OM, you have to go deep into the stillness. Go deeper.

The mind should be in the belly, the library is in the head. We should re-learn how to function from the belly, not from the head. Some years ago the Japanese looked into why thousands of their students commit suicide during their exams. It was a time when passing exams was extremely important. They found out that the students where working only from the head, the brain, and the brain could not cope with all this information pouring into it with no relief. The Japanese doctors found out that their hara (bellies) were empty; there was no cushioning for the information that was being received from the outside world. And in the end there was no cushioning, no nurturing or strength left in their bellies (hara). There was only fear in their bellies, because they were empty. When the breath centre (cauldron, in the lower part of the belly at the back of the belly) is full, there is no room for fear. Everything we do, we should do from the belly. We receive information and knowledge through the heart centre, (anahata). From the heart centre it travels down into the solar-plexus centre (some times know as the second brain, second only as it has to be developed) before travelling up into the brain. If we miss out this vital link within the belly, we cause problems for ourselves. When the belly is full there is expansion. If the mind is in the belly when the belly is full, the mind expands beyond itself, taking in everything. When we are completely full within the belly, when we sit in the belly, we have control over the mind. All feeling are felt in the belly, therefore if we are in the belly, we have control of our feelings, which means that we have control of our thoughts (the mind is made up of thoughts), which naturally leads to control of our actions. The amount of control we have depends on the amount of energy (prana) within the belly. That is why it is so important to breathe into the belly, and not to let all the pranic energy leave on the out breath. I often say condense into the heart charka, at the end of our Saturday morning meditation. It is best to be in the belly when we do this practise, not in the head. We feel our way into the heart centre, and feelings come from the belly. We can't think our way in. How far we travel inwards also depends on how still we are. Stillness is felt in the belly, not in the head. The inner journey starts in the belly. It is where we learn to soften; it is where we learn to feel, it is where we gather energy (prana). Be in the belly as you travel up and down the sushamna, be in the belly when you focus on the different chakras, and be in the belly as you wash the dirty dishes. Practise being in the belly at all times, it is simple, but hard to start with. Determination is very important and remember when you breathe into the belly; you are naturally bringing a little bit of yourself back to yourself. If the belly is full, it's fullness will wrap itself around the seed of fear, and like a seed of a tree that had been planted too deep in the ground will dissolve back into the earth. The seed of fear will dissolve back into pranic energy. Your everyday spirit, as I have said before, is part everyday feelings and part feelings from your soul. Gather your everyday spirit into your belly; sit in your belly, so that when the kundalini rises it will travel up with the kundalini. Then you will know yourself. If you liken yoga to a river, softening and feeling are the two banks of the river. The bed of the river is the belly and the current is the breath, the water is consciousness/life. The destination is the ocean of self-realisation, God-realization. What more can I say.

Get to know yourself.

The physical body is the mould for the astral body to move into. The astral body changes it's shape to what it enters. At the death of the physical body, the astral body will keep the form of the physical body until the soul's next birth. Then it will remould itself into the new physical body. As the astral body moulds it's self into the physical body, the causal body moulds it's self into the astral body. The causal body is so incomprehensible, so beyond the everyday mind. To comprehend your true self, you need to have an experience. Without an experience you can't comprehend it. The next question is, will you be able to accept it? It will not be for the mind to accept it, for you would have moved beyond the mind. You have to accept it! You are not the body, who the heck are you then. You are not the mind, you are beyond the mind. Today's mind (everyday mind) has only been with us since birth. Who am I? Keep asking yourself this question, keep looking inwards for the answer, you won't find it outside, it will come. Bring all of yourself back to yourself. It is a complete turn around if you want to know yourself. Your consciousness has flown outwards, in all direction. This outward looking has become habit, a habit that has been enforced through many lifetimes. But still, it is only a habit. A habit that you have created therefore you can uncreate it, if you wish. This habit can be likened to a comfort blanket of a child, and like a child who will one day let it drop, and no longer goes in search of it. For it has grown beyond the need of false security and false comfort. The child has grown in self-confidence. You too, must develop that same self-confidence. Let go of false comforts and false security. Be confident in yourself. Consciousness is forever expanding. There is no 'that's it, course completed'. There is no end to the expansion of consciousness; there was no beginning, so how can there be an end? Find that point of consciousness within you and you will know yourself. As I have said many times before, you have to be in, to expand outwards too know. Enlightenment/self realization is not the end, it is consciousness expanding. How can I put it, when we become enlightened for the first time, so to speak, we only know as much as we can hold within our point of consciousness at that time and we grow with it. This enlightenment/self-realization is held within our sub-consciousness. With our next re-birth within a human form, this enlightenment/self-realization that is stored in our sub-consciousness will sort of draw us inwards at every opportunity that comes our way. The more enlightened consciousness, so to speak, that is held with in the sub-consciousness, the more opportunities to re-awaken are drawn to us. Nothing that we have gained on our inner-journey is every lost. But we can add to the enlightenment/self-realization that is already stored within our sub-consciousness that we had gained in the previous life or lives. Enlightenment/self-realization is expansion, for it is consciousness, ever new, ever full within it's self. It's purity is beyond words, it's beauty, incomprehensible. There is no explanation for it, it just Is. It is the *Is-ness* within creation, and that is something else.

Do not try to fit consciousness into words, consciousness is consciousness.

Consciousness is beyond the comprehension of the mind, beyond the intellect.

You can not know consciousness, but you can feel it. Consciousness flows from God into all of creation.

Softening.

The Practise for Softening

We do three different formats of softening in our yoga classes. But you can just choose one for home practise. We start our yoga classes with slow deep breathing, into the belly. Yoga starts in the belly! This slow deep breathing in the belly brings us back to ourselves, it settles us down. After a few minutes, we move into the feet and soften the feet and all the toes, deep inside. Then we travel up into the knees, softening the knees, teaching the mind to feel, not think so much. Next we soften the thighs and the hips, remembering that the softer we become the stronger we become. Then we move into the belly, softening the whole of the belly and all its working parts, still further. Remember softening starts inside, not outside. Now we move up into the chest and like the belly, we soften the whole of the chest and all its working parts, feeling not thinking, moving inwards. Now we move into the arms, softening the whole of the arms. Remember, as we soften each part of the body, we stay there for a few moments or longer, feeling the softening in that part of the body as we let go. From the arms, we move down into the hands and soften the hands, the fingers and the thumbs. Next we move up, into the neck and throat, softening the neck and throat all the way through. Then it's into the face, softening the whole of the face, deep inside. Soften the mouth and the chin, soften the nose and the cheeks, soften the eyes and the forehead. We finish by settling into the softening for a few minutes before we start the yoga exercises. We do most of our yoga exercises laying flat on the mat. This is done so that the spine is kept straight. Many of us did not come to yoga till later on in our lives, when the body is not so supple. Softening opens up the body for the inner journey. Keep softening, keep feeling, don't hurry the softening, you are on your way.

When we have completed the yoga exercises that we practise on our back, we again soften, but this time we soften bigger portions of the body. We start by softening the hips, the length of the legs, then feet and all the toes. Then we soften the belly and the chest all the way through. Next we soften the whole length of the arms, the wrists, the hands, the fingers and thumbs. From there we move up into the neck and the throat, softening the neck and the throat, before we travel up, softening the whole of the face, the mouth and the chin, the nose and the cheeks, the eyes and the forehead. As we move around the body softening, we should feel the softening, not think it. This time round, takes us deeper into the softening. I usually say after each round of softening, that you can stay that way if you wish to, I would. The rest of us, have a nice little stretch.

After we have softened this time around, we turn onto our bellies to do our yoga exercises that we do laying on our fronts. When we have finished our yoga exercises, we again lay on our back and settle down into the softening. This time we start at the forehead. We soften the forehead and the eyes, the nose and the cheeks, the mouth and the chin. Then moving down into the neck and the throat, we soften the neck and the throat and the shoulders. Going down, we move into the arms, hands, fingers and thumbs, softening as we move inwards. Next we move into the chest and the belly, softening the chest and the belly. Then down into the hips and thighs, the whole length of the legs, feet and all the toes. Then we move back into the hands, fingers and thumbs and up the length of the arms, taking the softness to a deeper level. Then back into the shoulder blades, the neck and the throat, softening all the way through. Next we move into the face, softening the whole of the face. The mouth and the chin, the nose and the cheeks, the eyes and the forehead. A deeper softening, a deeper letting go. And we stay that way, till the class bell goes, or longer. We are inside, not outside. Softening is the key to the kingdom of heaven, which is inside of you.

Practise with the inner-breath.

The inner-breath is all around us and it comes in with the incoming breath. The inner-breath is life-force/pranic-energy, and in this practise, we try to keep *in* as much life-force/pranic-energy as we possible can, so that it all does not leave with the outgoing breath. This way we build up the inner-breath, making it stronger. With this practise we learn how to divide the incoming breath, so that we can keep hold of more life-force/pranic-energy, as the outgoing breath leaves.

We start practise by laying on the floor on our backs, with arms by our sides and legs straight with feet hips wide apart, and maybe a pillow to support the head. The spine is then kept straight in this position. We can also use a blanket if it is cold. When we have settled ourselves down with the softening and are ready to start the practise, we take the inner-breath into different parts of the body. First into the legs then up into the solar plexus, then into the chest, then neck and then up into the forehead. We then take the inner-breath down into the hands, then elbows to the hand and then upper arm to the elbows. We finish this practise by keeping the inner-breath in the belly, and mentally pushing it down into that space in the belly that I call the cauldron. We hold on to the life-force, for we are gathering it's energy for our inner-journey. When we move into each section of the body with the inner-breath, we stay there for a few minutes or so, filling each part of the body with the inner-breath. We do this twice; the second time round should be in deeper harmony". This practise should not only be done at class; it should become part of our everyday living. We should practise every day, twice a day, morning and evening. Maybe for five minutes at each practise to start off with, then slowly, it will come; we will natural practise longer. We will in time, find that we are doing the practise when we are not actually in practise. Also we will find that the feeling of the inner-breath moving through the body, or gathering in the belly, grows stronger and is in greater harmony. This practise is done to open up the body, and to prepare the body for when the kundalini rises. There are 72,000 gates within the body. If the gates are shut when the energy is released by the ascent of the kundalini. The released energy (the innate super-charged energy that is known as the kundalini), that has been asleep, so to speak, at the base of the spine, will just crash into the gates, rebounding and shooting off in all directions. This can have a very violent affect on the body and is not very pleasant. When the gates are open the life-force/pranic-energy that is known as the inner-breath and the super-charged energy know as the kundalini, passes through them like the wind through a flap. The deeper you go with the inner breath, the more open to Spirit. The inner breath takes you to God.

The practise of keeping the centre line clear.

After we have stayed in the belly gathering the inner-breath for sometime, we can move into the practise of keeping the centre line clear. We can stay as we are laying on the mat, or move into seiza (a kneeling position) keeping the spine straight. This practise takes us into the sushumna, which I refer to as the centre line. The sushumna is a column of energy within the spine, and it can be likened to a ladder of six runs, which leads, or opens into, is a better way of putting it, the seventh charka, enlightenment. At each run of the ladder, is a chakra. Each of these chakras is a vortex of energy; and are keepers of certain powers. When the chakras are not open, they pulsate and can be liken to a vortex-ring whose axis is a closed curve. From the base up, the first chakra is in the coccyx, know as the muladhara chakra, it is the root charka and it's element is earth. The second is in the small of the back (the navel area); this one is called the svadhistyana. It's element is water. Then we move up into the third, solar-plexus area, this chakra is called the manipura, and it's element is fire. Next is fourth, the heart chakra, called the anahata, and it's element is air. The throat chakra is next, the fifth, and it is called vishuddha. It's element is space. The chakra in the forehead, the sixth, is called ajna and is beyond the elements. The seventh chakra, which is above the sushumna, is the crown chakra called sahasrara which is beyond time, space and elements. After saying all that, I usually only refer to the chakras by their positions within the spine. It makes the practise easier; for we are not use to thinking and hearing in sanskrit. This practise is to keep the centre line (the sushumna, column of energy within the spine) clear.

When we start this practise, we first move into the forehead centre (ajna charka, charka six.) and then from here, moving inwards, we find the centre line (sushumna). We feel our way in. Now we start to move down the centre line, stopping at each centre on the way down. So down we go, keeping the centre line to the centre at the back of the neck,(vishuddha, charka five). Down we go again, into the centre between the shoulder blades, (anahata, charka four). Now down into the plexus centre, (manipura, third chakra) keeping the centre line, moving inwards, we move down into the small of the back centre, (savdhistyana, second charka). Then down, down into the coccyx centre, (muladhare, first charka, root charka). When we reach the coccyx centre, the root chakra, we start to move back up the centre line. Again, stopping for a few moments at each centre on the way up. We do not jump from one centre to the next; we travel up and down smoothly within the centre line, pausing for a few moments at each chakra. We do this practise in preparation for the ascent of the kundalini. When Jesus said the road is long and narrow, He was referring to the sushumna. At the end of our practise, we finish in the heart centre, (anahata charka).

The practise with the inner-breath is a practise to keep the cauldron, (that space in the lower belly, the breath centre) topped up with inner-breath/ energy, ready for the ascent of the kundalini. As well as keeping the energy paths through the entire body clear and opened. In time this practices will become a habit, a good habit, for we will naturally keep the inner-breath in the belly as we breathe. The kundalini's (super-charge energy laying dormant at the base of the spine) only purpose is to flow up the sushumna, opening up the chakras on it's way. It is the chakras that hold the different powers, but the kundalini is the key that opens them. After the kundalini has travelled up the channel (sushumna) any excess energy will then flow through the entire body. That is why it is important to keep all the energy channels within the body clear. This practise of moving up and down within the centre line (sushumna) is to keep it clear from blockages. The kundalini will only ascend when there is enough inner-breath (life-force/ pranic-energy) flowing into it. When the inner-breath is depleted, the kundalini will descend and remain dormant until the cauldron (breath centre) is again topped up. But remember all this is not possible without the softening.

The seed-mantras for the six charkas

The six chakras within the sushumna have what is known as a seed mantra, (a potent vibrational sound). The seed mantras for the chakras are as follows; travelling up from the base of the spine to the top of the spine. The first is the Coccyx, (muladhara chakra) it's seed mantra is *LAM*. The next centre is in the area of the spine known as the small of the back, opposite and just below the navel. This chakra is called the svadhistyana. It's seed mantra is *Vam*. The third is in the solar-plexus area of the spine. This chakra is called the manipura and it's seed mantra is *Ram*. The fourth is in between the shoulder blades and is know as the Anahata and its seed mantra is *yam*. Centre five is found in the spine, at the base of the neck. This chakra is called vishuddha and it's seed mantra is *Ham*. The next chakra, chakra six is at the top of the centre line(the sushumna) it is found in the centre of energy line that travels from the medullar, (situated at the centre of the base of the skull) to that point on the forehead between and just above the eye brows. This centre is known as the ajna chakra. It's seed mantra is *Om*. The seventh centre, the sahasrana charka is above the centre-line (sushumna). It has no seed mantra for it is beyond sound.

We start this practise by moving in to the centre-line (sushumna) through the coccyx centre, the base chakra, the muladhara, there, we mentally say the seed mantra for this chakra, *Lam*. We say the seed mantras mentally, for if we say them out aloud, the sound will pull us out. We would follow the sound out, instead of moving in. Then keeping to the centre line (sushumna) we start to move up, stopping at the next chakra, svadhistyana (small of the back) and mentally say the seed mantra of that chakra *Vam*. We do not jump from one chakra to another; we move gently and smoothly up and down the centre-line (sushumna), keeping it clear. So we move up the centre-line (sushumna), stopping at each chakra and repeating the seed mantra for that chakra. When we reached the top of the centre-line (sushumna), the forehead centre (ajna chakra), we then travelling back down, again stopping at the chakras and repeating their seed mantra, till we reach the coccyx, the muladhara charka. In this practise, we will at one point start to feel what I call a twinge as we stop at each chakra and repeat it's seed mantra. The more we practise, the stronger the twinges, the more we can pin-point each charka in the centre-line, (in the sushumna). This of course takes discipline and patients. Also, you might not feel a twinge but something else. We are all different, so our experience will differ. This practise can last 10, 15, 20, 30 minutes or longer and it is a practise that is best done on our own. For we have to find, our own rhythm. Also we can repeat the seed mantra once, twice or three times, whatever feels comfortable, but no more that three times. When we feel that we are ready to leave the practise, we move into the heart centre, the anahata chakra, without jumping, and settle in that centre before leaving.

Extra guidelines

When you enter the sushumna from the base, the muladhara chakra (coccyx) as you mentally say the seed mantra *Lam*, slightly slant the spine forward from the base, keeping the spine straight. This very slight movement helps to open the chakra. You do this slight movement at each chakra as you move up the centre-line (sushumna). Feel as if you are climbing a ladder. When you reach the forehead centre, the ajna chakra and start to move back down the centre-line (sushumna), move the spine backwards, again a slight movement, at each chakra. This helps the mind to focus on each chakra. So as you move up the centre-line (sushumna), it is a slight forward movement at each chakra, and as you travel down the centre-line (sushumna) the movement is a slight backward movement at each chakra.

A small gathering of Sensei's teaching on Jesus.

Quite often during Thursdays afternoon teas, Jesus and quotes from the Bible will come into the teaching. This is a small gathering of Sensei's teachings on Jesus, as I have understood them so far. I have added verses from the Bible that relate to the teachings.

Sensei has often said that, John the Baptist was Elijah, Jesus was Elisha.

From the Bible. 2 Kings Chp 2 v 9, *There Elijah said to Elisha "Tell me what you want me to do for you before I am taken away." "Let me receive the share of your power that will make me your successor" Elisha answered. V 10. "That is a difficult request to grant" Elijah replied. "But you will receive it if you see me as I am being taken away from you; if you don't see me, you won't receive it". V 11. They kept talking as they walked on; then suddenly a chariot of fire pulled by horses of fire came between them, and Elijah was taken up to heaven by a whirlwind. V 12. Elisha saw it and cried out to Elijah, "My father, my father! Mighty defender of Israel! You have gone!" And he never saw Elijah again V 15. The fifty prophets from Jericho saw him (Elisha) and said "The power of Elijah is on Elisha!" They went to meet him and bowed down before him.*

Sensei explains that Elisha was put into the condition that allowed him to receive the knowledge, the power from Elijah. Elijah was full, and when he gave a share of his knowledge and power to Elisha, Elijah was still full and Elisha became full. And, taken up to heaven by a whirlwind, represents the inner whirlwind caused by the ascent of the kundalini (potent energy that sleeps in lower part of the belly until it is roused and starts it's ascent by moving into the root chakra and traveling up the sushumna, a column of energy within the spine, striking each of the six chakras that are rooted in the sushumna, causing a whirlwind within each chakra as they fully open, until it opens into the seven chakra at the crown of the head (Sahasrara) If the soul is a realized soul and is leaving, it passes through the Sahasrasa. The Sahasrasa holds within, infinite consciousness, heaven, and is beyond time and space. Sensei also said that Jesus must have been a Kriya Yogi in his life before, and that He was a Kriya Yogi in His life as Jesus before He became a Christ.

From the Bible with reverence to Elijah being John the Baptist. Matthew chp17, v10. *Then the disciples asked Jesus "Why do the teachers of the Law say that Elijah has to come first?" V.11 "Elijah is indeed coming first", answered Jesus, "and he will get everything ready, V12. But I tell you that Elijah has already come and the people did not recognize him, but treated him just as they pleased. In the same way will they treat the Son of Man. V 13 Then the disciples understood that He was talking to them about John the Baptist.*

Sensei: John the Baptist died so that Elijah could appear at The Transfiguration. Elijah had to be at The Transfiguration for the prophecies to be fulfilled.

Luke chp9 V30. *Suddenly two men were with Him (Jesus). They were Moses and Elijah.*

Sensei has also said that Jesus Christ put His disciples into a condition that enabled them to enter into Him, into The Christ Consciousness, so that they could experience The Ascension. At The Ascension, they saw Jesus Christ ascend into heaven and while in that condition, they must have fully understood the meaning of His words "The Kingdom of God is within you". Sensei says that Jesus' heart centre (Anahata, unstruck sound) is permanently open. Pure Love flows continuously from the Heart of Christ, a stream of unbroken Love to all of Gods Creation. The Ascension of Jesus Christ has been watered down over the ages. The Ascension represents the Unconditional Love of Jesus Christ who spoke of the divinity within us all, with words like, "*What I can do so you can do*" and "*Heaven is within you*" or "*What you do to others you do unto me*". Jesus also said "*The one that sent me will come*". Sensei said that Sai Baba fulfils the prophecies that are written in the Book of Revelations including the mark on His thigh. Sai Baba also bears a mark on His side that represents the spear that was plunged into Jesus' side. Sai Baba fulfils all major prophecies.

Sensei has also said that the Old Testament is the foundation of the New Testament. Jesus came from the Old Testament into the New Testament. Without the Old Testament, how could there be a New Testament? Jesus' life as we know it, started in the Old Testament as Elisha, disciple of Elijah. You could say, Jesus is the enlightenment of the Old Testament.

Jesus.

Jesus

Jesus, like all Great Masters, threw off His childhood when He was fourteen. Fourteen seems to be the coming of age for God-men. When He left home, He first traveled to Egypt. There He met some Buddhist who recognized Him for what He will become. They told Him this, but also told Him that He would need to go to India to learn who He was. Jesus' so called lost years are now coming to light. In those years Jesus was taught how to manifest the powers He brought with him. To rekindle the knowledge that was held within Himself. Jesus was already a Realized Soul when he was born but He had to go and learn from others who He was, for Him to become a Christ. Jesus' birth tells that His birth was not due to karma, for He was born of a virgin.

When I was a young boy, I was always asking questions on what I had read about Jesus and His teachings in the New Testament, and also what I was taught. To me, something was missing. I could not back then say what was missing, but I knew something was, and I wanted so badly to find it. I would ask many questions and read the stories of Jesus over and over again. The key that Jesus gave to His disciple Peter (Matthew chp16 v19) became my prompter, my touch stone, is it this, is it that? The question came in many ways, but no answers came. Until I became a young man and then I had to travel to India to find them. The key that Jesus gave was the key to the inner-path, the path that leads to the kingdom of heaven, to self-realization, to God. The key itself is the softening, for you can't go in without softening. I cannot see how it cannot be this, and the more I read the New Testament the more sure I am. It is all there. That's why I say Jesus was a Kriya yogi (Realized Soul). As I practiced the teaching I had been give while I was in India, from both the Swami and the Japanese Master,

I could see Jesus' sign-posts along the inner-path. I slowly began to realize that what Jesus had done, I was practicing to do. Or I would read a passage in the New Testament and realize that I could also do that, or I could feel that. These are my own realizations, they came from inside, not outside. Too many sign-posts have been taken out of the New Testament, why?

Jesus said "What I can do, you can do", remember these words. These words are a big sign post, but you have to go in to feel them. Jesus became a Kriya Yogi (a Realized Soul) in His life as Elisha. Some people seem to talk about realization as if it is something you can buy in a shop. Jesus' teachings are universal and authentic. When I was a young man in India and I read that Jesus was buried in Srinagar in Kashmir, I felt the truth in those words, I did not think it. It is about time we took Jesus down from the cross. The soul that was born to Mary was a soul of a Kriya yogi (Realized Soul) on it's way to Christhood. You can't get closer to God than that. Although, God is closer than that to you. When you can feel, know and say without any fear of doubt, God and I are One. Then you have become a Christ. You have reached the highest level we can rise to while in human form, the Christhood. A Christ is full of humility and compassion. Swami Sri Yukteswar, Paramahansa Yogananda's guru was a Yogi Christ, and there have been others.

When He talked about the key to the kingdom of heaven, He was not talking about an actual key of a gate to the kingdom of heaven, which is somewhere out there. The key He talked about was the key of turning inwards to the inner-path to Christhood. We all have an inner-path. The paths may vary but the destination is the same. When the high priest asked him, and said unto him, Art thou the Christ, the son of the Blessed? And Jesus said "I am" (St Mark chp 14, v61-62). Jesus was talking about His Unity within God. Jesus never said He was the only Christ. When He said: I am the way, the truth and the light. and no one comes to the Father, except through me. He was talking from within and about, the Christ consciousness, not from a man called Jesus. Within every soul is a tiny spark of God. When the soul has evolved into a soul within a human body, the soul receives the key to the knowledge of God. For many more lifetimes the soul may still be outward looking, gathering experiences, experimenting until in one lifetime the soul feel something within, the soul turns inwards towards this feeling and touches the key, and it may be a few more lifetimes before the soul realizes what the key is. Then the inner-journey starts, slowly at first, but it will come.

Jesus' teachings on the inner-path.

When Jesus told His disciples The Holy Spirit would come to them. He was talking about the Destroyer of ignorance and Embodiment of spiritual wisdom. Know as Shiva in the Hindu Trinity and the Holy Spirit in the Christian Trinity. Jesus declared that He was a Christ when He said "God and I are One. His disciples also included women, Mary Magdalene, and Mary His Mother were to name but two. Women disciples were rare in those days. When Jesus said "The kingdom of heaven is within you". He was talking about the sahasrara, the crown chakra, (7th chakra) described by the Ancient Sages as 'which holds infinite consciousness, heaven and is beyond time and space.' No words can truly describe this. It is beyond words, that is why it has no seed mantra (sacred sound), for the sahasrara is beyond sound. It was there before creation. The single eye He talked about was the 6th chakra, the ajna chakra, the forehead centre. When this is open the body is full of Light. Creation came with the sound of OM. The sound of creation OM is the seed mantra (sacred sound) for the ajna chakra, the forehead centre, the single eye that Jesus talked about.

When Jesus said, "Follow me and I will show you the kingdom of heaven". Jesus was teaching the inner-path to God the Father. He was also teaching of the brotherhood of man. Mankind includes everyone. As I have said before, Jesus came to lift humanity to a higher level of consciousness. He took some of the negative karma of the world and placed it in His body. This act is beyond our comprehension. It was an act of Unconditional Love, Jesus' compassion flows without distinction, for He sees no distinction. But remember, Jesus too had to fight for Christhood. In The New Testament it talks about Jesus' forty days and nights in the wilderness, and it mentions and gives hints of other inner battles. Jesus' teachings have been watered down so to speak. They are taught on the worldly level but not on the inner-level, the soul level. The teaching is now based on logic, not on the inner knowledge that is felt. Learn to feel to the depth that Jesus did and walk the inner-path to Christhood, self-realization, God realization. Even in my life time the Bible has been altered, things have been added and things taken out. But there are still enough inner sign-posts to help us on our own inner-journey. There are sign—posts through out The Bible, from the Old Testament into The New Testament; Jesus came from the Old Testament. The prophets in the Old Testament also did miracles like Jesus, the differences between the prophets in the Old Testament and Jesus was that Jesus said "What I can do, you can do". He did not mean straight away! He was telling us that we all could walk the inner-path; it was not just for a select few. He showed the way for those who had eyes to see and ears to hear. Now the Father has come to teach this same message. Baba has said

"There is only one God; there are not different gods for each religion. It is the same God that listens and answers all prayers.

We are unfolding the path!
As we move inwards the path unfolds,
and the sign-post are there to let us know
we are facing the right way, and
going in the right direction.

It was a Saturday morning in January 2009 and the meditation session was coming to an end. Sensei had finished guiding us through the meditation practises, (that had not changed that much since he had started up the Saturday morning meditation session a long, long time ago). As usual, we heard him say "on your own then", as he got up to leave the dojo. Slowly we all got up in our own time and left the dojo. The next Saturday he did not come, nor the next, nor the next, although when asked (till we stopped asking him), he said he would come back, but we need time find our own rhythm, our inner rhythm. This was the first time we did not see. Howard once said laughingly to him, "I know why you do not come on a Saturday morning any more. It is because you like to go to the market with your friends for breakfast". Sensei said "No, that is not the reason. I want to see who will continue with the practise". That was the second time we did not see. One Thursday in May 2010 he stopped coming for afternoon tea. That was the third time we did not see. A few weeks after that in connection to what we thought was to afternoon tea, he said firmly "I have got to go". It seemed a bit strange for him to say that at the time. That was the fourth time we did not see. There where many, many things that the people of the dojo and of the town did not see. We thought he left us suddenly with out any warning, until we saw.

Sensei left his body on
Monday 9th August 2010
by a yogi practise called
Jal-samadhi

Printed in Great Britain
by Amazon

54394653R00066